DRAWN

D0851917

DATE DUE

AUG 3 0 2000

MAY 1 4 2001

MAY 2 9 2001

JUN 1 9 2001

JAN 1 3 2002

JAN 3 0 2002

JUN 1 3 2002
AUG 1 5 2002
OCT 0 8 2002
Oct 1 S
NOV 1 2 2002

MAY 2 2 2000

Palos Verdes Library District

Sunset

ideas for great

BABY ROOMS

By Christine Olson Gedye and
the Editors of Sunset Books

Sunset Books ■ Menlo Park, California

Sunset Books

vice president, general manager:
Richard A. Smeby

editorial director:
Bob Doyle

production director:
Lory Day

art director:
Vasken Guiragossian

Staff for this book:

developmental editor:
Linda J. Selden

copy editor:
Marcia Williamson

design:
Barbara Vick

page layout:
Susan Bryant Caron

illustrations:
Susan Jaekel

principal photographer:
E. Andrew McKinney

photo director/stylist:
JoAnn Masaoka Van Atta

production coordinator:
Patricia S. Williams

10 9 8 7 6 5 4 3 2
First printing January 2000
Copyright © 2000 Sunset Publishing
Corporation, Menlo Park, CA 94025.
First edition. All rights reserved,
including the right of reproduction in
whole or in part in any form.

ISBN 0-376-01046-0
Library of Congress Catalog Card
Number: 99-63574
Printed in the United States.

For additional copies of Ideas for
Great Baby Rooms or any other Sunset
book, call 1-800-526-5111. Or see our
web site at: www.sunsetbooks.com

Cover: A beach theme ties together this cozy
room; handpainted furniture gives it a
personal touch. Interior design by Laurie
McCartney for babystyle.com. Cover design
by Vasken Guiragossian. Photography by
E. Andrew McKinney. Photo direction by
JoAnn Masaoka Van Atta.

A room is born

While there are shelves of books available on how to care for babies, very little is said about how to create the rooms in which they spend their first few years. This book is meant to fill that gap. A nursery is not just a younger version of a child's room. It has its own special set of considerations. How do you keep it safe for a curious baby? Stimulating, but also restful? Convenient for the adult caregivers, but comfortable for the little one? You'll find the answers to all of these questions in this book, as well as ideas and inspiration for creating a special, very personal first environment for your baby.

Many professionals, businesses, organizations, and homeowners assisted us by providing advice and information, or by opening their doors to our photo crew. We would especially like to thank Sherri Peake of Bellini in Bellevue, Washington; Go To Your Room in Seattle; Cartan's Kids Stuff in San Ramon, California; IKEA; Safety for Toddlers of Kirkland, Washington; Barbara McQueen Interior Design; the Environmental Home Center; the Washington Toxics Coalition; the U.S. Consumer Products Safety Commission; and Lighting Design Lab in Seattle. Credits for specific designs and products are listed on pages 110 to 111.

contents

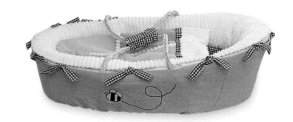

4

a dream coming true

WILL IT BE an undersea motif, complete with a coral-reef mural and tropical-fish curtains? Or perhaps a soft, vintage look with an heirloom bassinet, chenille cushions, and a stenciled floral border? If you're like most parents-to-be, you start fantasizing about the nursery well before you settle on a name for the baby.

The famous "nesting" instinct that kicks in during those months of anticipation has a lot to do with it. Every parent wants the newest member of the family to be cozy and comfortable, and it seems prudent to take care of as many preparations as possible before there's an actual baby to tend.

But there are other reasons the nursery awakens the interior designer in everyone. Decorating this room is more fun than decorating any other room in the house, and usually much less stressful. You can make a splash with colors and patterns you probably wouldn't consider using in other rooms, or try your hand at painting a mural or stitching some decorative pillow covers. For some parents, this is the chance to realize their own fantasies of a child's dream room. After all, it may be the last time the room's occupant isn't going to whine about your choices.

On the practical side, outfitting a nursery can be relatively inexpensive compared to redoing a kitchen, bath, or living room. Many parents start with a borrowed crib, secondhand toy shelves, and a simple bureau that doubles as a changing table.

However, well-chosen top-of-the-line furniture can last through high school, making the investment worthwhile.

Whether you're a novice on the decorating front or a practiced hand, you'll appreciate this book's step-by-step process. Use "A Planning Primer" (pages 7 to 27) to take stock of what you have, decide what you'll need (before baby arrives and later on), and put it together in a space that will be able to serve a growing child. The photo gallery in "Great Baby Room Ideas" (pages 29 to 81) offers pictures of dozens of finished rooms that will inspire you. Finally, "A Shopper's Guide" (pages 83 to 109) is a reference to help you choose everything from cribs and changing tables to lighting and floor coverings. The pros and cons of all the options are spelled out clearly—you need only decide which pattern or style or color will make your baby's room a dream come true.

A PLANNING PRIMER

I**F** your baby is still on the way, it might be hard to see much past delivery day. But it's important to think about the future as you plan the nursery. **WHERE WILL THE BABY SLEEP** in those first weeks of night wakings? Will the room function as both play space and sleeping quarters, or do you have a family room where most of the toys will be kept? Will the room eventually be shared? Or might the baby later move out of the nursery to make room for a new sibling? **CONSIDER YOUR BUDGET AND TIMETABLE** as you work out the room's ideal layout and look. "A Shopper's Guide" (pages 83 to 109) can help you estimate the costs. **PLAN FOR SAFETY** as you use this chapter to develop your design. The in-depth checklist on pages 20 to 21 will help you make sure the nursery is hazard-free from floor to ceiling. **HOW WILL THE BABY RESPOND?** On page 27, we provide a glimpse into what babies would like to see in a nursery—as well as what they actually can and cannot see.

the master plan

THE EXCITEMENT *of impending parenthood brings with it not only a strong nesting instinct, but also an extra measure of impulsiveness and, inevitably, a little forgetfulness. Here a well-thought-out plan comes to the rescue. So pull out a notebook, a pencil, and a tape measure, and get ready to lay the foundation for a great nursery.*

How feathered a nest?

Your child's room will serve many functions over the next few months and years: changing station, sleeping quarters, scribble art gallery, and center stage for a developing imagination. The more you think through its likely uses and incarnations now, the less likely you'll have to revamp the room at each of your child's developmental stages.

Though baby stores would have you believe otherwise, a newborn's real needs are few: soft clothing, breast milk or formula, diapers, a car safety seat, and a snug place to sleep.

For many new parents, the sleeping place ends up being in or near their own bed—at least for the first few months, when the baby is waking up several times a night. If the baby is close at hand, Mom or Dad can respond to his cries before they escalate to a panic, and the whole

Once the rocking-horse fabric was chosen for this baby boy's room, the rest came together easily. A matching wall border banded with trim gives the architecturally plain room more character; the window valance lifts the pattern higher. Sponge-painted walls will disguise the inevitable smudges and dings.

This nursery is situated just off a Tuscan-inspired living area, so the parents opted for sophisticated earth colors. The garden border is a washable wallpaper framed with strips of trim for an illusion of greater depth. The fabrics used are tied together with a sage, cream, and terra-cotta color scheme.

feeding goes more smoothly. (It's not surprising that many seasoned parents say the best furniture investment they could have made prebaby was a king-size bed!)

Why go to the trouble of putting together a nursery? First, the "co-sleeping" arrangement doesn't work for every family. Some parents decide to put a daybed in the nursery so that one can spend feedings in comfort in the baby's room while the other gets a good night's sleep. Other families find that a comfortable rocking chair or armchair in the nursery is sufficient to handle an infant's night wakings.

Of course, regardless of how the night routine is worked out (and most won't settle on a solution until weeks after the baby is born), the baby will still need a place to sleep during the day, a place for diaper changing, and a place to store clothes, bedding, and a few simple toys. And keep in mind that, while you might be content to buy only a few special outfits and playthings, between shower gifts and packages from well-meaning friends and relatives, your baby will almost certainly amass a generous wardrobe and toy collection in need of homes.

Looking down the road a few months, the nursery will need to accommodate the delicate knees and hands of a crawler, a developing brain that thrives on change and stimulation, and—all too soon—the wobbly gait of a toddler. Safety, cleanliness, functionality, and comfort (for both baby and parent) must come together as in no one other room.

For some expectant parents, that means buying a full suite of furniture, painting an elaborate mural on the walls, and acquiring curtains, crib linens, and lamp shades to match. For the Shabby-Chic inclined, it may mean combing antique stores for a vintage rocking chair and a beautiful old braided rug to complement a distressed-finish crib. Another couple might opt simply to roll a fresh coat of paint on the walls, borrow a crib from a friend, and move in a set of drawers and a bookshelf from other parts of the house. Both the baby's and the parents' needs can be met with any of these treatments, and with a whole range in between.

To arrive at the plan that suits your family best, take a close look at the three factors that will become the parameters of your nursery project: budget, time, and space.

A little ingenuity brought eclectic charm to this budget nursery. Mom's childhood bookshelf showcases books and toys; ceramic knobs become a fanciful hanging rack. An old chifforobe (above) displays treasures safely out of reach. Decorative paper plates above the crib (above, right) catch the baby's eye without compromising safety.

Decide on a budget

Babies are expensive. The essentials—food, medical attention, child care, clothing, and education—add up quickly. With those expenditures on the horizon, it's wise to sit down and decide how much you want to spend on the nursery.

First, know that you can put together a fine room on a bare-bones budget—as long as you have plenty of time (to visit garage sales and to comparison-shop) and creativity (with painting or sewing) and an eye for pulling together disparate elements. Luck figures in, too. If you have friends who can lend you baby furniture and trimmings, consider yourself charmed.

If you are on a budget, be sure to let your fingers do some walking—through the phone book, through catalogs, and over your computer

keyboard. The Internet is increasingly useful as a source of baby goods. For more on the pros and cons of various shopping options, see "A Shopper's Guide," page 83.

Even if your motto is "the sky's the limit," try to come up with a ballpark figure of what you'd like to spend. You'd be surprised how quickly the different elements can add up. It's not hard to walk into a high-end baby store and drop $6,000 on furniture and bedding alone. Tack on another $2,000 for a rug, window coverings, fresh paint, a mural, and accessories. And that's just the room. You'll also be buying a stroller, a highchair, and a car seat. The list will grow, and so will the bottom line.

So, as you read through the rest of this chapter, keep running lists, preferably in a notebook you can refer to while you're shopping. One list is "To Do" and the other "To Buy." As you flip through catalogs, visit stores and garage sales, and consult with contractors, you'll get a sense of how much you can expect to spend on each item. Juggle the dollar amounts so that the total stays within your budget. And don't forget, you won't need everything right away, and sometimes it helps to spread out the expenses. The crib, for instance, can wait until the baby is three or four months old if necessary (and you might decide to skip it if co-sleeping works for your family).

Watching the timetable

Are you a dedicated do-it-yourselfer, eager to spend spare hours feathering that nest? Or do both you and your partner work crazy hours? Is your baby due many months from now, or fairly soon? The more time you have, the more you can spend shopping for great bargains, doing your own painting or sewing, or sprucing up secondhand treasures. (Check "A Warning for Pregnant Women," page 19, before undertaking any projects that might involve harmful substances or fumes.)

If there are a few months before the baby arrives, but shopping time is limited by a hectic life-style, your best bet may be one-stop shopping at a full-service juvenile-furnishings store. Such specialty stores often have more helpful staff than sold-in-the-box baby superstores, and they can guide you through all

the decisions so you end up with coordinated pieces. They can also often refer you to muralists and other specialized contractors who can complete the look for you. Two catches: these retailers often carry the highest price tags, and the high-end furniture you order from them can take months to arrive.

If, on the other hand, you've found yourself with just a few weeks to go—or if the baby is arriving earlier than expected—the minimalist approach is not such a bad one. Prepare the room by cleaning it thoroughly and hanging basic blinds (painting and carpeting should really be done a few months in advance to allow fumes to dissipate). Then make sure you have accounted for the basics (see box, next page). You'll probably find that your actual needs aren't nearly as great as you thought they would be.

Richly printed fabrics in burgundy and navy combine with dark wood furniture to make a sophisticated statement in this boy's nursery. (Homeowner's hint: buy enough fabric to make twin-size bedding to coordinate down the road.) Existing neutral walls and carpet were unchanged.

NURSERY ESSENTIALS

Not sure what you'll need for Junior? The good news is, not everything right away. Following is a list of the basic necessities, an overview of must-haves. "A Shopper's Guide," pages 83 to 109, goes into more detail on each of these subjects. (Keep in mind that this list does not include non-nursery essentials, such as a car seat, a front-pack carrier, clothes, diapers, bottles, blankets, and so on; consult a baby-care manual for a complete list of accessories.)

A PLACE TO SLEEP. Unless you want the baby to sleep with you, for the first few months this will probably be a bassinet, cradle, Moses basket, or large pram. Some people simply cushion a drawer or clothes basket with towels and blankets, and let the baby snooze there until it's time to move to a crib—at around three months, or whenever the baby starts rolling over.

STORAGE FOR SMALL CLOTHES, TOYS AND BOOKS. "Small" is the key word here. All those little one-sies, booties, and blankets will become a jumbled mess in typical large bureau drawers and closets. Miniature board books will be swallowed up by most bookshelves. Stuffed animals, on the other hand, are often large, and they multiply on every birthday and holiday. Consult pages 94 to 96 for smart storage strategies.

A PLACE FOR DIAPER CHANGING. A contoured pad snapped onto a hip-height dresser or desk is a sensible solution; the pad can be removed once the diaper phase is past (by two to three years for most children), and you'll be left with a perfectly usable piece of furniture. Or you can bypass furniture altogether and simply fill a basket with wipes, diapers, creams, and a foldable waterproof changing pad that can be used on a bed, floor, or couch in any part of the house.

A DIAPER BIN. If you opt for a cloth-diaper service, it will probably provide this, so hold off on purchasing one until you know. If you choose disposable diapers, you'll need a bin with a sealable top (more on this on page 91).

A NURSING CHAIR. It might be an old family rocking chair or your favorite old overstuffed armchair. Whatever you choose, make sure it will be comfortable to sit in for long periods and the arms are generously padded. Many mothers opt to do their feedings lying down on a daybed in the nursery instead; it gets passed along to Junior when he graduates from the crib.

AN ELECTRONIC MONITOR. These listening devices allow you to go about your business in the rest of the house (or even the garden) without losing touch while the baby snoozes in his room.

A CRIB MOBILE. Brightly colored objects hanging in baby's view are a prime diversion in the pre-sitting, pre-toy-grasping months. Make sure you choose one that captivates baby from his point of view: looking up from below. Also, the bolder the contrast, the greater the appeal will be in the early weeks; black and white or primary colors are popular with babies for a reason.

Which room is right?

When you select a room in your house to be the nursery, there are several factors to consider. You'll find it's convenient to be near a bathroom, especially if the baby's room is diaper-changing central and lacks a sink. If you choose a room that's close to your bedroom, you will be able to respond quickly to your newborn's nighttime cries. Of course, if you plan to have your baby sleep in your room at night, this is less of an issue; you might prefer the convenience of having the daytime napping place and changing table closer to wherever you spend most of your waking hours.

While it may seem obvious to choose the smallest room in the house for this tiny occupant, that's not necessarily the best long-term solution. Children end up spending much more time in their bedrooms than most adults do; their rooms become a play space, a study, and a place for entertaining friends and hosting sleep-overs. Make sure there is space for your child to grow, unless your plan is to use the smallest room as a nursery for the babies and graduate them into bigger rooms as siblings come along.

Another set of considerations involves noise. Excessive street noise can disrupt sleep, and soundproof windows or storm windows are a help only if you don't need fresh air to circulate in the room. While you don't want to have the room so quiet that your baby becomes oversensitive to sound, it may be better to choose the bedroom farthest from the street. It's also wise to have the nursery away from the living and dining rooms if you're likely to entertain during evening hours.

Another question to consider: Will the room be warm enough in the colder months? If there are drafts, consider storm windows. You may also want to install an adjustable-speed ceiling fan, which can moderate extreme temperatures at

This nursery can still function as the guest room it once was— and also let a parent recline in comfort during night feedings. Masterful painting effects tie it all together: the wooden crib is finished to match the wrought-iron bed, and trellis murals echo the bed's headboard design.

any time of year, depending on how the blades are turning, and is safely out of a child's reach. (A bonus here: babies are easily transfixed and calmed by the sight of slowly rotating fans.) While you're at it, check how many electrical outlets the room has. It's ideal to have at least one on each wall, since you won't want extension cords trailing around a toddler's room.

If you can, choose a room with plenty of natural light. South-facing is ideal. Don't worry about the room being too bright for daytime sleep: blackout blinds are always an option. The advantages of having a cheerful, naturally lit room will far outweigh the cost of any window coverings you may find necessary.

Overcoming fundamental flaws

If you are fortunate enough to have a large, regularly shaped room with plenty of light, and walls and floors that are in good shape, congratulations. You can easily fit in a crib, dresser, rock-ing chair or daybed, toy shelf, and maybe even some extras like a chifforobe or toy chest.

On the other hand, if you have a small or awkwardly shaped room or windows that open to an oppressive scene or let in little natural light, you'll have to be more selective. Fortunately, most architectural deficiencies can be overcome with clever decorating techniques.

SMALL ROOMS. Paint the walls, trim, and furniture in the same light color to create the illusion of more space. Minimize clutter. Can the child's toys live in the family room? Can "diaper central" be in the bathroom? Use small-scale furnishings and a small print in wallpaper and fabrics. Built-in furniture takes up the least amount of floor space. Use wall or ceiling light fixtures rather than floor or table lamps; they take up less space, and they're safer, too.

DARK ROOMS. Use warm, pale colors, such as yellow and pink, to brighten rooms that face north or east. Position mirrors to reflect as much

A large closet with charmingly painted sliding doors conceals a built-in changing table and plenty of storage for clothes and toys; cupboards on top store items not currently in use. The faux window on the right is framed with painted rope for an added sense of dimension.

CREATING A LAYOUT

Well before you go nursery-furniture shopping, draw a plan of the room on graph paper. Using a ¼" = 1' scale, map out the outer dimensions of the room, noting doors (and their direction of swing), windows, closets, and so on. Be sure to indicate the placement of outlets, light fixtures, wall switches, heaters, and vents. Note window dimensions, as well as their height from the floor, plus the measurements of any door frames, window trim, baseboards, or chair rails that might affect furniture placement, window treatments, or wall-covering purchases.

Once you've done the basic floor plan, play around with furniture placement. One initially time-consuming but worthwhile way to do this is to cut out pieces of paper representing the size and shape of the furniture you will be using in the room. The following standard measurements should give you a place to start in cutting out these scaled furniture templates.

Crib: 30" x 54"

Changing table: 15" x 34"

Chest of drawers: 18" deep x 42"–60" high x 31"–36" wide

Rocking chair/glider: 24"x 30" (plus rocking space)

Bookcase: 9"–12"deep x 2'–6' wide

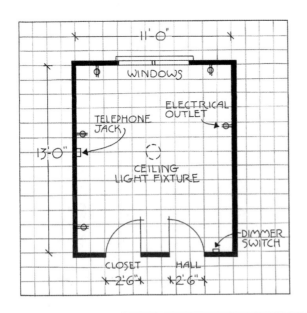

SOME FURNITURE ARRANGEMENT TIPS:

- Place the crib first, as it is likely to be the largest item. If you have the space (and your crib that has two drop-down sides), it's handy to have the crib approachable from either side. Otherwise, a corner placement is both safe and space-saving.

- Place the dresser/changing table close to the closet so that everything is handy at changing time.

- Both the crib and the changing table should be away from windows, radiators, heat or air-conditioning ducts, and any pull cords or draperies.

- Maximize open floor space so your baby will have plenty of room to crawl and later play. Think train sets, somersaults and roughhousing.

- Utilize vertical space for storage by choosing tall bookcases or high wall-mounted shelves. A bracket shelf mounted a foot below the ceiling is a great spot to stash growing collections of soft toys (see page 66 for an example).

- Place electrical devices (monitor, music player) near outlets to avoid the use of extension cords.

- Children love to look out the window; make one accessible with a bench or window seat. Be sure the child cannot open the window, and consider using reinforced glass or a safety gate in front of the window.

- If you are planning on a mural, make sure your layout takes it into consideration (you won't want furniture to block it). Whether you have a hardwood floor or wall-to-wall carpet, you can use throw rugs to define areas: Use one in front of the changing area, one near the toy and book shelf, and one at the base of the crib. A round or oval rug can soften a room with lots of angular furniture and corners. Be sure to use nonskid pads under all area rugs; you may even want to use several pieces of double-stick tape if your floor is especially slippery.

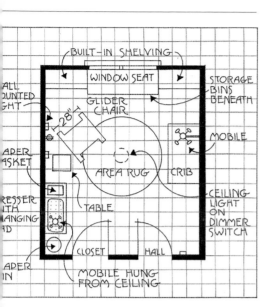

BUILT-IN SHELVING
WINDOW SEAT
STORAGE BINS BENEATH
GLIDER CHAIR
WALL MOUNTED LIGHT
28"
MOBILE
PAPER BASKET
AREA RUG
CRIB
DRESSER WITH CHANGING PAD
TABLE
CEILING LIGHT ON DIMMER SWITCH
CLOSET   HALL
PAPER BIN
MOBILE HUNG FROM CEILING

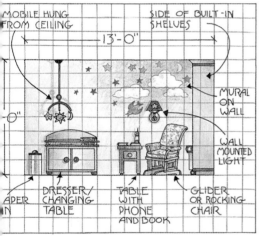

MOBILE HUNG FROM CEILING
SIDE OF BUILT-IN SHELVES
13'-0"
MURAL ON WALL
WALL MOUNTED LIGHT
PAPER BIN
DRESSER/CHANGING TABLE
TABLE WITH PHONE AND BOOK
GLIDER OR ROCKING CHAIR

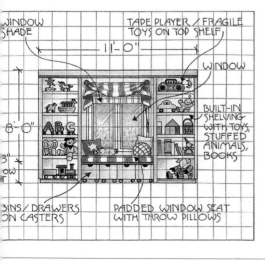

WINDOW SHADE
TAPE PLAYER / FRAGILE TOYS ON TOP SHELF
11'-0"
WINDOW
BUILT-IN SHELVING WITH TOYS, STUFFED ANIMALS, BOOKS
8'-0"
ABC
3"
BINS / DRAWERS ON CASTERS
PADDED WINDOW SEAT WITH THROW PILLOWS

light as possible. Cover the windows with simple sheer panels that provide privacy without sacrificing natural light. And, of course, install a high-powered ceiling fixture (on a dimmer switch) for general lighting, and wall lamps for the changing table and rocking chair.

OVERLY LARGE ROOMS. Make a big nursery seem snugger with warm, rich tones. Bold and/or large-print wallpaper will have a shrinking effect. Use a darker shade to visually lower the ceiling, and bring this color down to a picture-hanging rail or border high on the wall.

AWKWARDLY SHAPED ROOMS. For disproportionate rooms, remember the magic of stripes: Vertical lines have a heightening effect in short areas, whereas horizontal lines will make the room seem wider or longer. If the room has a dormer ceiling along one wall, put the crib there; as long as the baby isn't standing, there's no risk of his bumping his head on the sloping wall. If the dormer slopes all the way to the floor, build in low toy shelves for the bottom two feet and deem it a "get down and play" area; put the changing table in the middle of the room where the ceiling is highest.

An old-fashioned baby carriage with a bassinet attachment makes a convenient first bed, as it can be wheeled indoors or out without disturbing the baby. The bassinet can be lifted from the base and replaced with a seat when the baby is sitting up.

Sharing a room

Though this family was willing to give up their guest room for a nursery, the older sister insisted on sharing her room with the new baby. The striped wallpaper has a traditional look, but with a whimsical watercolor touch. A braided chenille rug softens the old fir floor.

Sometimes sharing a room is the only option: there simply isn't another bedroom to offer a new baby, or the extra bedroom has to be used as an office for a work-at-home parent. But sometimes sharing a room is the option of choice, either for an older sibling who wants the baby's company at night (yes, it really does happen!) or for parents who wouldn't dream of separating their twins or triplets.

With multiples, the challenge is mostly a space issue: how to fit in two or more cribs and enough storage space for all their belongings. Consider some of the layout tips outlined in the "Small Wonders" section (pages 58 to 63), and take a close look at "Clutter Control" (pages 76 to 81) for clever storage ideas. Unless you have help, you'll rarely be changing more than one baby's diaper at a time, so one changing table is probably sufficient. If you don't insist that the babies wear matching outfits, they can swap clothes, giving you more flexibility and requiring less clothes storage space.

Making space for a baby in an older sibling's room may seem more daunting. Won't the baby wake up the older child? What about all those toys that are choking hazards for a crawling baby? And if one is a boy and one a girl, how do you handle the decor?

First, your child may be a deeper sleeper than you suspect; many preschoolers surprise

their parents by sleeping right through most of a baby's night awakenings. If that isn't the case for you, have your newborn sleep in a bassinet or portable crib in your own bedroom or another nearby room for the first few months, or until he no longer needs to eat at night. This is handier for you anyway, and will help the older sibling ease into life with a baby. Or set up a camping pad and sleeping bag at the foot of your bed or in another room for those nights when the baby's cries wake your older child.

On the toy front, some parents simply move all too-small-for-baby toys into a family room, where it is easier to monitor play. Another solution is to restrict small toys to the shared bedroom, but never allow the baby to be there unsupervised. A gate on the bedroom door that only parents and the older sibling can operate will achieve this once baby is moving around the house on his own. The advantage to this strategy is that the older child has a greater feeling of keeping his "turf" and has a place to go if he doesn't want to be bothered by the baby.

As for the boy/girl decor dilemma, think of it as incentive to create a room that lets kids be kids instead of macho boys or dainty girls. Primary colors help achieve this, although soft

blue and yellow are gender-neutral colors in a subtler palette. Or choose ivory or white walls with wood floors and furniture, and let the children's toys and bedding be the accents.

Finally when it comes to compromises, the best way to preserve the peace at this stage is to go with the older child's preferences, as long as they don't pose a safety hazard.

Even a small room can be shared with a newborn. In this Minnie Mouse-inspired room, a cradle fits in at the base of big sister's bed.

A WARNING FOR PREGNANT WOMEN

The nesting instinct might give you a hankering to repaint the nursery walls or strip an old toy chest down to the original wood, but expectant mothers should channel that energy in other decorating directions.

While today's latex paints are safer than the arsenic-, lead-, and mercury-containing paints of yore, it's safest to leave painting projects to a spouse or good friend and vacate the house while the work is being done. Choose low-toxin, not just low-VOC (volatile organic compounds) paints. Also, make sure there is plenty of ventilation both during and after the job; ideally, let the house air out for a few days

after painting before the mother-to-be returns. Have any painting done as far in advance of the baby's arrival as possible so residual fumes and gases have time to dissipate. The same goes for installing new carpets with backings or pads that could give off harmful toxins.

If refinishing furniture or stripping wood is in your plans, that, too, should be left to someone other than the mother. Most chemical paint removers are highly toxic, and the chance of absorbing harmful additives from the paints you are removing is too great a risk for a pregnant woman to take.

a safe haven

CREATING A HAZARD-FREE *environment is a top priority in nursery planning. Well before you're expecting it, your baby will be rolling and reaching, then pulling up and climbing. Sometime before your baby is six months old, look at his room from a safety perspective.*

A custom-made gate swings open easily for adults, but keeps triplets from wandering into trouble.

GET DOWN ON YOUR HANDS AND KNEES. Look around. You'll probably see outlets, electrical cords, dangling curtain cords, and a host of other obvious hazards. There are dozens of others that aren't nearly as obvious. Use this section as a checklist for baby-proofing the nursery.

Some parents turn over this job to professional baby-safety experts. To find a pro in your area, contact the International Association for Child Safety at 1-888-677-IACS. Remember: no matter how many safety devices you install, there is no substitute for vigilant supervision, especially in the first two years of life.

CRADLES, BASSINETS, AND CRIBS. Make sure cradle and bassinet stands are sturdy and stable. Read the crib safety specifications on page 85. For maximum security, place the crib in a corner, away from windows and window cords. As soon as the baby can sit up, lower the mattress to the bottom level and remove all bumpers, pillows, and soft toys that could possibly be used for climbing. Toy bars should be attached to the middle of the back wall of the crib so they can't be used like rungs in a ladder. Any fitted crib sheet should have elastic all the way around and should be generously cut to allow for shrinkage; fitted sheets that come loose present a choking hazard. Pillows, quilts, and thick comforters pose a suffocation risk and shouldn't be used in the baby's first year.

WINDOWS. Put locks on windows and remove all furniture and potential "step stools" from under windows, or add bars or a shatterproof film. Imported vinyl miniblinds may

contain lead, so be sure to buy those labeled lead-free. Keep long curtain and blind cords out of reach by wrapping them around cleats high on the window frame; on blinds, choose wands instead of cords when possible.

FURNITURE. Make sure all furniture is sturdy and splinter-free, with rounded edges and no protrusions or loose screws. Assume it will be climbed on: bolt any tall or tippy pieces to the wall. Toy chests should have safety hinges and air holes.

CHANGING TABLE. Buy a changing pad with a concave shape to nestle the baby and discourage rolling over while you're changing him. Many changing pads come with straps; even if your baby submits to wearing the uncomfortable things, it is not a permission slip to turn away from the table for even one moment while the baby is on it. The changing table is second only to the bathtub in terms of required vigilance. Keep all creams and baby-care items out of the baby's reach. Overhead mobiles must be beyond grabbing distance, and the diaper pail should have a child-proof lid.

ELECTRICAL AND HEATING. Push furniture in front of as many outlets as possible; install self-closing outlet covers (see page 109) on the others—outlet plugs can become choking hazards. Keep electrical cords out of reach by fastening them to the wall with cord sleeves or colored duct tape. Simple winders can take up excess cord. Use overhead fixtures instead of tip-prone lamps. Cover radiators and baseboard heaters with screens.

ALSO:

- Steer clear of toys and objects with small parts or ribbons, cords, or loops that could choke a baby. Keep siblings' toys out of reach and pay attention to age recommendations on toys, especially those marked for children over three.
- Use safety mirrors or treat mirror backs with safety film to prevent shards of glass from forming during breakage. Do not hang mirrors or heavy pictures above a child's crib.
- Do not leave a night-light on all night: preliminary studies show a relationship between myopia and excessive exposure to nighttime light during the first two years of life.
- Discard all plastic bags and packing materials, and keep them out of baby's reach.
- Install smoke and carbon monoxide detectors in or just outside the nursery.

From left: A discreetly placed video camera helps parents monitor kids in cribs. A cleat wraps excess window-covering cord, which otherwise might be a choking hazard. An out-of-reach door latch makes the closet a safe storage place.

a look that will last

ONCE YOU'VE ASSESSED BASIC NEEDS, *it's time to think about the look and feel you want to create for your baby's first environment. This is where color, pattern, texture, furniture style, and all the decorative details come together.*

CHANCES ARE, you already have a starting point for the look of your baby's nursery. Maybe you've chosen country pine furniture that would work with a farmyard mural and chambray bedding. Or perhaps the view out the nursery window suggests a nautical theme or a garden scene. You may have found a charming bedding set, wallpaper border, or area rug that can be a foundation for other choices. Or perhaps you've always known you wanted a sunny yellow nursery with a sky blue ceiling, and all the details will flow from that color scheme.

Some families take a cue from the other rooms in the house and build from there. Whether you favor traditional furniture or contemporary, coordinated decor or a more eclec-

The warm, rich colors in this nursery-in-waiting will work for a boy or girl. The Old English alphabet border is at once sophisticated and playful, appealing to both baby and parents. The animal-print lithographs on the wall come from an old book; an antique rocking horse was reconfigured into a lamp.

tic look, you will be able to find baby furnishings that echo the style you've already established.

If, however, you are truly starting from scratch, look for visual ideas everywhere. The handiest place to start is this book's photo gallery, "Great Baby Room Ideas" (pages 29 to 81). Each room pictured is filled with ideas you can borrow. Then peruse catalogs and magazines and visit stores, collecting photos, swatches of fabric, and paint chips or wallpaper samples that are pleasing to your eye. Most likely, a pattern will emerge—a color scheme, a theme, a look, a feel. Continue to build on it.

Later, when you're ready to make some decisions, go through your collection of swatches and photos and narrow your choices down to the pieces that work well together, or to the design or color scheme you've settled on. Glue or staple these items to the inside of a manila folder, and put your room layout inside. Carry this "room collage" with you whenever you shop so you can avoid costly mistakes and mismatches.

Many parents decide that a nursery—more than any other room in the house—beckons for a full-fledged mural.

What could be more cheerful and evocative than a storybook scene painted on the walls? A word of caution before you plunge into this potentially expensive pursuit. A one-note, four-wall mural throws to the wind the cardinal rule of nurseries: flexibility. Furniture is harder to arrange when the wall decor is permanent. Curtains and bedding can be trickier to select, unless you choose those first and get the muralist to work with them. Finally, you will be much more hesitant to paint over a mural that you or your child grows tired of than you would be to hang a new poster.

If, however, you decide that now is the time and the nursery is the place, an experienced muralist can help you work through some of these issues.

Referrals from friends are the best bet; boutique-like nursery-furnishing stores are a safe alternative. Whomever you hire, be sure to look at examples of previous work—ideally the originals, or, if that's not possible, a wide range of photos. Is it the style you had envisioned? Ask what type of paint was used, and how nontoxic and washable it is. If your child takes a permanent marker to it, will the artist come out and fix it? Finally, have postcards, a book, or other visual references to give the artist a sense of what you're looking for, and ask to see sketches or a scale drawing before he begins.

Boy or girl?

Many expectant parents like to take a wait-and-see approach on finding out the sex of their baby. Does that mean the nursery decor has to be put on hold as well? Not at all.

In fact, many thoughtfully designed rooms these days are fairly gender-neutral, as parents try not to foster traditional boy–girl stereotypes. Many color schemes work for either a boy or a girl: yellow, green, bold primaries, and neutrals like earth tones and whites. Even blue, once thought to be the province of boys' rooms, has become a familiar background color in girls' nurseries. And with so many gender-neutral themes to choose from—nature, animals, the alphabet, and so on—there's no reason to limit your baby's room to something overly boyish or girlish.

In praise of simplicity

The final consideration to keep in mind as you dream up your baby's nursery is this: you will have to take care of it. Crib linens will have to be washed—often—and the delicate cycle won't do it. There will be spills and spit-ups on the floor, the rocking chair cushion, and just about every piece of furniture. The walls will suffer fingerprints and errant scribbles. So, as you're making purchasing decisions on everything from sheets to wallpaper to window coverings, think in terms of what can be easily cleaned and maintained and what will be able to hide stains, bumps, bite marks, and scratches. After all, you'll want to spend as much of those first years playing with baby—not cleaning his room.

This room's decorative painting complements the themed crib bedding, but its bold colors and stripes will easily transition to different motifs over the years. A wavy line dances around the room, echoing the scalloped edge on the crib quilt (used as a wall hanging). Natural-finish furniture with rounded lines softens an otherwise vivid room.

The challenge in this spacious nursery was making it cozy.
Creating a sitting area made the room an intimate
gathering spot for the whole family, and ficus and ivy
leaves invite the outside in. The full-size daybed with trundle
was ideal for the baby nurse in the early months, and later
will make slumber parties a breeze. The round ottomans
shift around the room easily for seating, and store toys as
well. The handsome wooden trunk provides more storage,
and serves as both coffee table and play surface.
A built-in bookcase is ideal for toy and book storage;
the top shelf displays family collectibles. French doors
open onto a sunny patio.

Turquoise, orange, and red are sure to brighten any child's room. Equally gender-neutral are the plaids, stripes, and swirls on the cushions for the built-in bench. Padded fabric cornices jazz up easy-care louvered shutters and bring the lively colors higher.

FROM THE BABY'S PERSPECTIVE

Just how much your baby appreciates his new environment is directly correlated with his age. Up until two months, he sees clearly only what's within 8 to 12 inches of his face, and even then he doesn't see in color. Bold, high-contrast patterns and simple shapes are the most eye-catching, followed closely by anything in motion. That's why you'll find lots of black-and-white toys and mobiles in the infant section of toy stores. Not until a baby is six to nine months old will he be able to clearly see and focus on things both near and far, and in a full range of colors.

Does that mean a black-and-white-striped crib set is the best choice? Not necessarily. A baby's vision and interests change so rapidly in the first six months that such bedding would quickly become a bore. Also, the crib isn't the best place for intense stimulation. A few well-chosen toys and pictures against a tranquil backdrop are all a newborn really needs.

If you have a collection that's easy to rotate, so much the better; your baby will appreciate a change of scenery every so often. Hang a mobile with changeable attachments above the diaper area—a great place to have some distraction. Or attach a few bulldog clips to a clothes hanger over that area and attach a changing array of soft, colorful toys. Don't for-

get, the baby will be gazing at these from below; position them accordingly.

Wall hangings and other decorative elements can both give the baby something to look at and lend the room a finished quality. Here are some ideas.

■ Look in school-supply stores for colorful borders and laminated posters. Use a temporary adhesive to mount them on the wall.

■ Hang a pair of clear plastic box frames on a wall, and change the contents frequently. Use enlarged family or baby photos, illustrations from old children's picture books, or an older sibling's drawings.

■ Hang a kite or wind sock from the ceiling.

Finally, remember that vision is only one of your baby's senses; be aware of the textures, noises, and scents in his environment as well. Are the sheets soft to the touch? Have you made a space on a high shelf for a portable stereo to provide cheerful tunes during the daytime or lullabies at night? And what about a safely elevated bud vase containing a single flower—for sweet scent and for color?

THIS POPULAR MOBILE COMES WITH HIGH CONTRAST CARDS THAT CAN REVERSE TO MORE DETAILED DESIGNS, AND THEN CAN BE REPLACED WITH COLOR DESIGNS, AS THE CHILD'S VISUAL ACUITY SHARPENS.

GREAT BABY ROOM IDEAS

In "A Planning Primer," we laid the practical groundwork for your baby's nursery. Now it's time to picture the room's look and feel. This photo gallery will provide ideas and inspiration to help you do just that. From folk art to French provincial, from pastel pink to bold primaries, you'll see dozens of different approaches. THE FIRST TWO SECTIONS of this chapter focus on rooms as a whole—what qualities unify each space and make it work both aesthetically and practically. Subsequent sections focus on special challenges: small rooms, sharing a room with a sibling, making the room comfortable for all who use it, and, finally, solving the storage problem. AS YOU BROWSE through these pages, look not necessarily for entire plans you can duplicate, but for pleasing color combinations, creative ways with paint or fabric, interesting uses of furniture. Take notes and flag pictures as you go; chances are, you'll take away several ideas you can use wholesale, and dozens of others you can personalize.

great baby room ideas

tying it all together

MOST NURSERIES have the basics: a crib, a place to change diapers, storage for toys and clothes, and a light overhead. But every once in a while you come across a room that has an extra quality that makes you say "Ahhh, yes." In some cases, it's a beautiful but unexpected color scheme. In others, it's a feeling of family history. In many rooms, what evokes that response is a certain harmony, a common theme that unifies the elements.

That's not to say that one character dances across everything from the sheets to the wallpaper to the lamp shades. While this is perhaps the simplest and surest way to achieve a cohesive look, these rooms can actually look too pulled together, and lack interest. Rather, rooms with high "ahhh" factors have a freshness about them that is decidedly free of most of the media-hyped images. In the examples here, the visual themes are more along the lines of American folk art, a sunny garden, French country design. They are

Spring-loaded hinges on this toy chest keep fingers pinch-free. Mural details are brought below the chair rail, where a darker background color will camouflage smudges.

playful. Imaginative. The elements in the room blend, rather than match. There's just the right amount of contrast. And the magic, by and large, is in the details: a lavish light fixture, a vintage toy collection, handpainted dresser knobs, a beautifully hung print.

The happy side effect is that these nurseries are as soothing and pleasing and joyful to the parents as to the babies. And given the amount of time Mom and Dad are likely to spend in the room, that is definitely a goal worth pursuing.

The folk-fanciful birds that decorate these walls were inspired by a pattern on the mother's own baby blanket; garage-sale furniture was handpainted with complementary motifs. The wardrobe's pole and shelves hold all the baby's clothing and blankets, freeing the room's closet for grown-up storage.

An inviting sitting room off the sleeping area houses an armoire for clothes, a window seat with storage space under the bench, and (out of view) a television cabinet, toy shelves, and a walk-in closet.

Topiary wallpaper with a picket-fence border, white wicker furniture, and airy toile fabric throughout create a sunporch feeling that will grow with the child. The wicker bed can sleep a nanny or older sibling—and eventually the crib's graduate. Shallow bracket shelves and a rolling cart keep essentials handy at diaper-changing time. When the diapering stage is over, the dresser top's elevated sides can be removed.

There's nothing babyish about the folk-art motif in this small nursery. All the furniture (except the crib) was designed by the baby's mother. Wall shelves display collectibles. A tray on the changing table holds three lidded boxes with ointments, cotton balls, and other necessities. The handmade lidded hamper and trash bin keep little hands (and the family dog's paws) out of trouble.

The mustard, sage, and burgundy quilt inspired the room's gender-neutral color scheme. Behind the chicken-wire doors of a barn-shaped wall cupboard is a collection of antique toys. Farmyard-animal pegs keep hats and other essentials within easy reach, while a stool functions as a small-scale side table.

Toys are stored in open crates with handles that make it easy for a toddler to tote them around. A rolling cart provides mobile storage. The crib's bumper was co-quilted by the baby's mother and grandma.

In the changing area,
painted-on clotheslines
are "strung" with
tacked-on clothespins
holding fabric scraps
and antique linens.
The changing table
itself was new, but
its distressed finish
gives it a softer, more
farmhouse-like look.
A real clothesline and
more pins lift fabric
remnants to form a
soft valance for the
wood slat blinds.

Trompe l'oeil painting, inventive furnishing details, and vintage fabrics combine to create a sunny, country feeling. Real birdhouses— one hanging, one on a stand—blend humorously with two-dimensional versions. An old baby scale has been converted to a low occasional table, at perfect height for the mini-armchair next to it.

The inside of this old corner cabinet was painted pink, and the glass on the doors was replaced with chicken wire, also pink. On the right, a painting by the artist-mother bears the child's nickname. The doll bed and footstool are heirlooms, contributing to the room's warm sense of family history.

The antique crystal chandelier, purchased in Paris, was the inspiration for this French country room. A linen veil hangs with hook-and-loop fastener from a crown painted by the artist-mother. A Manet print in an elegant little frame is hung with upholstery cording and a silk tassel from the picture rail.

Simple but grand toile curtains hang from wrought-iron rods set well above the window tops to accentuate the high ceiling. The dresser, a family piece, was stripped, whitewashed, distressed by heavy sanding, monogrammed, and then protected with wax. Generations of family memorabilia decorate the dresser top, along with a jug of fragrant lavender. The small rocker was crafted by an uncle.

murals
and color

PERHAPS THE SIMPLEST WAY to transform a room is with a coat or two of paint. Even a subtle color change will provide an appreciated freshness. But with a little extra effort, paint can create a magical transformation. Consider using two colors sponged or ragged on for added depth. Or add a thin pinstripe border just below the ceiling, or a contrasting color on a chair or picture rail.

Start by choosing a color you're naturally attracted to, rather than one that seems baby-appropriate. Test it out on a large piece of primed cardboard and move the sample around from wall to wall at different times of day. Consider it with the flooring, trim, bedding, and curtains you have. If your favorite color packs too much punch for all four walls, use it on just one or two, with a more subdued tone on the remaining walls.

Stencils and rubber stamps can yield beautiful decorative touches even for beginners. Try out your design on paper first. And color need not be limited to paint on the walls. Consider the furniture in the room as an extension of your canvas.

If a mural holds strong appeal for you, consider limiting it to one wall. Also, the less babyish a mural is, the longer it will be appreciated. The themes with the most longevity are general ones, such as nature, animals, sports, or transportation, as opposed to those that revolve around one particular character. Unless you possess confidence with a paintbrush, you'll probably want to hire a muralist. See page 24 for some hiring tips.

Colorful Mexican fabrics are attuned to the vibrantly painted furniture. A swan-shaped rocking toy was redesigned into a rocking gecko.

A midpregnancy dream of "happy geckos" inspired this color- and critter-filled nursery. The mother hoped the bright hues and playfully abundant use of pattern would encourage her child's creative side.

*Babies appreciate
vivid colors at least as
much as older kids.
The view from this
crib includes sea
creatures peeking in
through portholes on
one wall and a jungle
scene on the other.
Bright yellow paint
frames each painting.
(Stuffed toys and
pillows, which can be
suffocation hazards,
are removed when the
baby is sleeping.)*

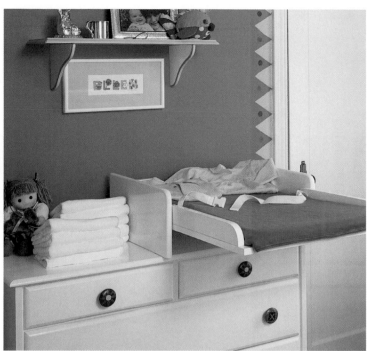

In this space-saving unit, the changing top flips closed when not in use; it will lift off when no longer needed. Handpainted knobs customize the piece in the style of the wall treatment. Baby treasures sit out of reach on a bracket-supported shelf.

A recycled glider got a face-lift with a hand-sewn slipcover; buttons were painted to match mural colors. A baby book is kept handy for quick scribbles while nursing, and the telephone is within convenient reach. The small round table is free of potentially hazardous corners.

A child's toys blend right in with the bright hues in this room. The crib and the melamine corner dresser unit, formerly white and gray for an older sister's room, were painted in bold planes of gold and purple. The rounded cabinets are streamlined as well as corner-free. The area rug was made to order by a craftsperson spotted at an art fair.

A tall storage cabinet ties in all the room's colors. Playful-looking, delicate lamps are set safely high. The floor lamp, placed out of reach behind a chair, illuminates bedtime stories.

Here the walls get a lift not from paint, but from a canopy of striped fabric hung to create a circus-tent look. The theme was chosen because it's playful, colorful, not strictly feminine, and leaves lots of room for the imagination. Crib bedding was sewn from a reissue of vintage fabric, while the circus prints came from an old "Bozo the Clown" record album. To the left of the crib, a child's armoire (a flea-market find) has hanging space and drawers to store clothes and bedding.

An old storekeeper's chest with glass-fronted drawers holds diaper supplies near the top and a collection of older sisters' shoes, which lies in wait for the youngest.

A tiger appears on the wall at child's-eye level; the child-sized chair and stuffed menagerie reiterate the jungle theme.

High ceilings give headroom when a giraffe strides across the wall. Dark colors on the mural's lower half will hide inevitable fingerprints. Animal-print fabric ties the furniture into the mural's theme.

Though primarily yellow and blue, the room has mural-related accents of barn red on the lamp, the edge of the dresser top, knobs, chair buttons, ball pillows, and pull-out bins under the window seat. The left compartment under the bench is open for a heat vent.

A huge storybook moon looming in the corner creates a floating-through-space feeling in this hey-diddle-diddle nursery. Delicate metal "aircraft" hanging above the crib spring up and down with a parent's gentle pull— an artistic alternative to the more familiar crib mobile.

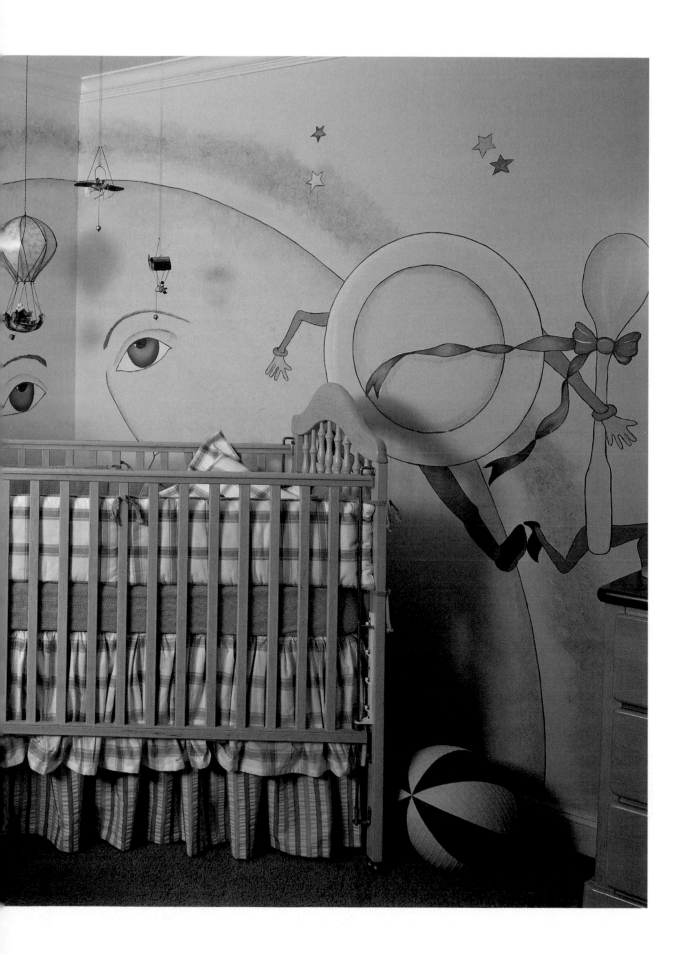

This whole-room
mural sets the stage for
high-seas adventures.
The closet's sliding
doors were finished
with automotive
paint so they can
take many years of
opening and closing.

Manipulating
perspective in the
mural makes this
room seem larger than
it is. The receding pier
was personalized with
names of businesses
of family friends.

This room started with a colorful collection of quilted
animal wall hangings, the toy chest, and the cloth palm tree.
The muralist created a safari environment in the same
cartoonish style, then added the amiable-looking giraffe.
With a little imagination, the shapes of the painted clouds
also read as animals.

A combination of
drawers and shelves
in the changing area
concentrates most of
the storage at one end
of the room, freeing
up floor space for
play. The mural was
painted with this
furniture placement
in mind.

Padded wall
hangings give the
mural a three-
dimensional look.

Curtain fabric with a "Mary, Mary, Quite Contrary" motif inspired the mural here. Three-dimensional gateposts and the path winding toward a distant cottage give the small room an appealing sense of depth. The lattice-trimmed, built-in corner cabinet provides storage while taking up little floor space.

The muralist watered her paint significantly to achieve the soft, almost translucent colors; the previously faux-finished wall made a complementary background. Real fence pickets were sanded down and nailed onto the wall before painting to provide a realistic touch.

The Italian countryside, long a favorite destination of the parents, set the tone for this fresh-air mural. The painting also incorporates a few details from the mother's favorite childhood nursery rhymes—such as the Jack-be-nimble candlestick on the trompe l'oeil shelf, which also displays painted alphabet blocks representing the family names.

The mural is carried onto the toy chest, across the ceiling, and into an adjacent bathroom (not shown). This continuity, along with the openness of the sky and the diminutive size of villages on a distant horizon, visually expands the small room. Though the colors are soft, they are stronger than babyish pastels, and will easily "grow" with the child.

Friendly pairs in a Noah's-ark mural give this nursery a

cheerful quality. By limiting the mural to one wall, the

parents gained more options for rearranging the furniture.

A wall unit makes efficient use of space; eventually, the

changing surface will be replaced by a shelf.

The starry fabric of the bedding, chair, table covering, and window relate to the mural in color but not content. The parents made a conscious effort to limit the ark theme to the mural and remain open to other patterns and motifs throughout the rest of the room.

small wonders

THINK OF IT THIS WAY: a small room is cozy, which is ideal for a baby. That doesn't mean that small spaces don't have their challenges, but most of them can be overcome.

First, clutter is a big no-no: keep a give-away bin handy for all the little clothes and toys your baby doesn't really need. Can most of the toys and books be stored in the family room? A rocking chair or glider is a true space hog; consider putting it in the master bedroom or living room.

Always choose the most efficient option when you're looking at furniture: a dresser that doubles as a changing table, a bookcase with adjustable shelves. Also, make sure the piece is simple in design and small in scale. Before you order anything, measure the furniture and the room very carefully, and prepare a to-scale layout of the room (see pages 16 to 17). By pushing furniture against the walls, you'll maximize open floor space. Draw in as much natural light as possible with a strategically placed mirror.

The muted, monochromatic color scheme simplifies the small room. An armoire keeps clothes used on a day-to-day basis handy; the closet stores items the child will grow into.

Simplify your color scheme: choose one pale and subtle color to use on walls, furniture, window coverings, and bedding. Perk things up with a wall hanging here, a pillow there. When choosing fabrics, use small-scale prints (checks and dots are good) or rich textures.

Finally, don't forget to go vertical. Draw the eyes up with stripes on the walls or curtains. Bring window coverings right up to the ceiling, even if the windows stop well short of it (see photo on page 23). High-mounted shelves will achieve the same purpose.

This room's coastal theme was inspired by the mother's childhood; natural light floods the room, contributing to the outdoor atmosphere. Floor space was maximized by placing furniture against the walls; vertical stripes and the stencil detail near the ceiling draw the eye up. The dresser and the toy chest were handpainted to picture both the family dog and the room's current occupant.

Situated in one of the master bedroom's already ventilated walk-in closets, this nursery is handy not only to the parents but also to the bathroom. (The extra bedroom is freed up for use as a home office.) Built-in shelves store toys; bamboo trim glued onto their edges maintains the safari motif. The animal-print fabrics and rug, handpainted drawer pulls, and a folding screen develop the theme further. "Mosquito netting" softens the closet's cedar lining.

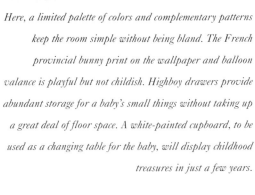

Here, a limited palette of colors and complementary patterns keep the room simple without being bland. The French provincial bunny print on the wallpaper and balloon valance is playful but not childish. Highboy drawers provide abundant storage for a baby's small things without taking up a great deal of floor space. A white-painted cupboard, to be used as a changing table for the baby, will display childhood treasures in just a few years.

A small corner in any room can become a big source of entertainment. Two shatter-proof mirrors are bolted to the wall at crawl-right-up level. A colorful pad on the floor makes it a comfy place for the baby to keep herself company.

A small-scale room
calls for appropriately
scaled furniture. The
birdhouse-inspired
shelf holds small books
and mementos. The
tall but shallow table
provides display space
without blocking the
wall's mural; a picket-
trimmed box holds
diapers, wipes, and
a pad for on-the-floor
changes.

Having a place for
everything minimizes
clutter in a small
room. Books are
stowed in the rattan
drawers on the left,
clothes in the dresser
under the changing
table. The chifforobe
holds shoes, blankets,
and extra lotions; its
low mirror has a
space-expanding effect,
and thrills the baby at
playtime.

great baby room ideas

peas
in a pod

SHARING A ROOM may seem like second-best from a
parent's point of view. But ask most young children, and they'll rate it
tops. Oh, sure, there will be tough moments—like when the baby
wakes up crying and rouses the other—but these issues can always be
worked out with a bit of inventiveness (see pages 18 and 19 for ideas).

For now, there's the challenge of creating a room that works for all in-
volved. If you have multiple babies, the task is easier: the occupants are less
opinionated than an older sibling would be. From a practical standpoint,
which items do you really need two of? Two cribs definitely. But one changing
table, one diaper bin (emptied frequently) and one well-organized dresser
should suffice initially if space is limited.

When it comes to the nursery's decor, do you want a "matched set" look,
with identical cribs, bedding, and toys? Or do you want to take a mix-and-
match approach? Several factors may figure in: Are the babies the same gender? Identical or fraternal? Do you
prefer an organized look, or a more
eclectic setting?

When the shared room involves
an older sibling and a new arrival,
it's more a matter of carving out
space for the newcomer. Take cues
from the one who is old enough to
speak his mind. Rearrange to accommodate a crib, a changing table and some baby toys and books.
If he's reluctant to welcome baby
into his room, choose the least in-
trusive corner for the crib, and
have the changing area in the
bathroom.

*Sisters share this small
room done on a tight
budget. The baby's
crib and dresser were
previously used by
her older sister.*

*Paint perks up the
walls, closet doors,
and a consignment
wicker chair; the soft
colors are tied together
in the curtains made
from sheets that match
the twin bedding.
Until sleep routines
were established, the
baby slept in a
portable crib in the
family room, closer to
the parents' room.*

Fabrics were chosen in advance of the babies' birth to suit whatever gender combination arrived (two boys and a girl). The awning-style window toppers complement the garden picnic theme of the mural and accommodate the arched windows; the scalloped lines are repeated on the cribs and changing units. A full-length couch at the end of the room allows the whole family to enjoy story time together.

With triplets, organization is the name of the game. This custom wall unit, designed and fabricated by the father, makes simultaneous diaper changes a snap for Mom, Dad, and nanny. The vertical cabinets below store a diaper bin and laundry hamper for each child, while drawers store all their clothes (the room has no closet).

Cherry pairs are a fitting motif for this twin girls' room in red, white, and blue. A bracket shelf running high on two walls efficiently displays their two-of-each toy collection. The crib previously used by an older child was impossible to duplicate, so a mix-and-match approach was taken with the furniture—giving the room a fresh, individual feel.

A sepia-toned Western scene, inspired by a similar painting in the father's childhood room, captivates the two boys who share this room. The bandana-like bumper ties, the footstool's retro fabric and other decorative details continue the idea. The masculine-looking Arts-and-Crafts-style furniture carries out the Western motif, and will last well into the next generation. When the younger boy outgrows his crib, a matching twin bed will become the lower unit of a set of bunk beds.

Twin girls share a room that, though feminine, is not
babyish. Romantic balloon shades are lined with blackout
fabric for nap time. A slipcovered chair and ottoman,
previously used in another room of the house, are comfy
enough for mom to snooze on at night. The floral-motif rug
was discovered at a flea market. An open closet displays
the girls' clothes, hats, and shoes.

comfort counts

IN THE BABY'S FIRST YEAR especially, most parents' top priority is sleep—for everyone in the family. For the baby, that usually happens in a crib or, early on, in a bassinet, pram, or cradle. Some families find co-sleeping in the parents' bed is what best assures a restful night's sleep. Whatever you decide, be sure the sheets on the bed are extra soft and securely tucked under, and that only thin blankets are used—or better yet, a warm sleeper and no blanket at all. Thick comforters pose a suffocation risk in the first year of life and are best used as decorative wall hangings or as floor blankets.

Just as important is the parents' comfort in the nursery. Where will you recline during those middle-of-the-night feedings? Do you have somewhere to sit while the baby plays on the floor? Yes, you'll want to be down on the floor with him as much as possible, but there will be times when you just want to sit in a comfortable chair or rest on a soft bed or couch.

Placing a cradle right next to the parents' bed was to make midnight feedings easier; the tiny newborn still prefers the coziness of a Moses basket, so it is set inside the cradle.

A rocker-glider is as comfortable as a medium-size chair can get, especially for nursing while sitting. But if space allows, consider putting a daybed in the nursery. It can provide a great way for both parents to get a better night's sleep: the one who is up to feed can lay down while feeding the baby, and the other is hardly disturbed at all. During the day it's a cozy place for story time. (For more information on cribs, bedding, and rocker-gliders, see those sections in "A Shopper's Guide.")

For something altogether different: a round crib with a high canopy draped in white eyelet is a feminine fantasy. The nearby bench doubles as a toy chest.

Originally brought in for the baby nurse, this twin bed waits for its future occupant. Meanwhile, caregivers lounge there while the baby plays on the floor. A unique frog-shaped toy chest complements the sea-creature theme.

Once the centerpiece of a guest room, the elegant queen-size wrought-iron bed stayed on in the room's nursery incarnation and set the tone for the decor. Though sometimes still used for visitors, the bed is mostly a luxurious comfort zone for nights when the baby needs company.

With closet doors removed, a double-size daybed fits nicely in the closet space and doesn't crowd the room. Most of the baby's clothes are in a dresser (not shown), but some hang from a pole above the bed. There is more storage under the bed and on a closet shelf obscured by the swag, made from sheets that match the bedding. Bumble-bee napkin rings decorate the curtain tiebacks.

Draping a mosquito tent over a newborn's crib ties into the mural's outdoor theme (it will be removed once the baby is rolling over). The painting's most engaging elements are low on the wall, where the baby can appreciate them. Simple linen bedding suits the room's restrained nature theme.

A crescent moon cradle rocks the baby to sleep in this dreamy, star-studded nursery. A child-size wing chair welcomes an older sibling at story time, while a matching parent-size chair is more than adequate for nursing sessions. Wall-to-wall lapis blue carpet is inlaid with gold stars.

clutter
control

NOTHING DETRACTS from a room's potential as quick-
ly as clutter. A baby's belongings, though small, are many: tiny socks,
dozens of diapers, an armload of blankets, and toys, toys, toys. A messy
space is inefficient and can be hazardous.

The best solution, of course, is to start by getting rid of any excess. At the
very least, get it out of the nursery, or at least out of sight. If the clothes or toys
are outgrown, give them away or store them on a high shelf in the baby's closet
or in the basement. Also, keep a large, clear plastic bin in the closet for toys
that you "rotate" off the shelves in your baby's room every month or so.

Design solutions can make a big difference on the neatness front as well.
Start with a thoughtfully planned closet—one that has child-scale hanging
space, plus extra drawers, bins, or shelves. A shoe holder with clear pockets
hanging on the back of the closet door is a great place for booties, socks, hats
and other items likely to get lost in a big drawer. A changing table with drawers underneath keeps diapers, wipes, and creams handy but out of sight.

*An open closet means
no doors to pinch
fingers, and allows
the twin girls to help
pick out their own
outfits. Shelves,
drawers, and an
extra pole were built
in for added efficiency.*

Be creative in solving your storage dilemmas. Can it be hung
from wall pegs? Do you have an
armoire in the house that can be
relocated to the nursery? Can you
mount shelves into a recess in a
wall or across a corner? Consider
open baskets and bins for storing
toys—they make it easier for you
and your child to identify what
goes where and to get it there
with ease. For more storage ideas,
see pages 94 to 96.

*A custom-built unit
houses a cabinet com-
plete with mini-fridge
and microwave for
storing and heating
bottles. Baskets are
mounted on drawer-
like glides that keep
them from falling out.
The unit will eventu-
ally move to the play-
room, where it will
keep snacks handy.*

A family-heirloom washstand was treated to a coat of paint to match the walls, then topped with a snap-on contoured changing pad. The drawer keeps diapering supplies close at hand, while toys above entertain the baby during changes.

Walls can provide valuable storage and display space when shelves with pegs are hung. The out-of-reach space is ideal for precious mementos.

A distressed-finished armoire houses books, toys, and framed photos, as well as shoes, hats, and other accessories. Tall and narrow, it makes good use of vertical space in this small room. The doors can be closed for an even tidier look.

A sturdy wall unit
bolted to studs in the
wall and painted a
vivid red holds small
toys and books now,
and is large and
versatile enough to
house evolving
collections throughout
childhood.

A narrow wall space
between closet and
bathroom doors is
efficiently used with a
toy chest/bench below
and wall-mounted
shelves above. It's also
an eye-catching place
for a pony parade.

A flea-market-find
cabinet was spruced
up with fresh paint
and flower details; it
holds the mother's
collection of glass
animals and other
delicate items. The
cabinet has safety
latches and is bolted to
the wall. The arched
doors on the right open
to a deeply recessed
cabinet with pullout
drawers for toys not
currently in use.

A SHOPPER'S GUIDE

BY NOW you've probably established an idea of the overall look you want your baby's room to have. But how do you pull it together? From bassinets and dressers to lighting and flooring, this chapter will provide the information you need. THE OPTIONS today are much more varied—often more sensible and, in most cases, much safer—than they were a generation ago. Traditional changing tables have been replaced by longer-lasting dressers with removable changing tops; cribs now meet strict safety guidelines; and old-style rocking chairs have evolved into comfy rocker-gliders. Also, there are as many different prices for any given item as there are places to buy it; being a savvy shopper can pay. LAST BUT NOT LEAST, health and safety concerns are ever more important in parents' buying decisions. We hear more each year about the effects of hazardous products and materials on small children, and we must make fully informed choices. Let this chapter be your guide.

Cribs and Cradles

COZY, SAFE BEDS FOR LITTLE SLEEPYHEADS

When it comes to the night-time routine, not all families start with a crib. Most babies spend their first months sleeping in something smaller and cozier, such as a cradle or bassinet, that can be set up in the master bedroom for convenience during night feedings. And some parents take their baby into bed with them from the start and find the closeness both convenient and rewarding for them and comforting for the baby (if you're considering this arrangement, called "co-sleeping," discuss it with your pediatrician as there are risks associated with it). By the time a baby is rolling over, it's time to move to a crib.

Beds for newborns

While smaller beds aren't really necessary, many parents find they are easier to move from room to room during the first sleep-heavy months. Others buy or borrow a cradle or bassinet so they can put off the purchase of an expensive crib until they find out whether or not co-sleeping works for their family. Unlike cribs, these little beds are not regulated for safety features, so check them over carefully before you buy.

CRADLES are like miniature cribs on rockers. They're usually made of wood, measuring about 18" × 36", and are too heavy to move around easily. Because they're larger than most bassinets, they can be used longer—until just before a child begins to sit up, at about five months (which is why

you'll want a substantial mattress—at least 2 inches thick). They are also the most expensive of the four types of newborn beds, ranging in price from $120 to $350, including bedding. Many families have an heirloom cradle that has been passed from generation to generation; sometimes parents buy a new one, intending to start a tradition.

A BASSINET is a stiff, woven basket that sits on a stand. (Ideally, you can lift it out of the stand to carry it downstairs.) Most come with a hood, which is handy for shading the baby from light during outdoor or daytime rests. Bassinets are lighter and slightly smaller than cradles, and can be less expensive; prices range from $40 to $550. Make sure the stand is sturdy and locks securely into position to prevent folding while in use. If the stand has casters, you can push the unit back and forth to lull the baby to sleep; check that the wheels are substantial and roll and swivel smoothly. As with cribs and cradles, the mattress should be firm and fit snugly in the basket. A shelf in the lower part of the stand is handy for storing extra blankets.

A cradle's side-to-side motion soothes the baby into slumber; a rocker lock stabilizes the cradle once the baby's asleep.

A MOSES BASKET (see top photo on page 86) is the least expensive of the newborn beds ($40 to $250), but by no means the least desirable. It's woven of corn husks and has relatively soft sides; it can even be packed into a large suitcase for travel to Grandma's house. While not likely to last generations, a decent-quality Moses basket will last for the first few months for several babies.

SIDECAR SLEEPERS (see bottom photo on page 86) are a response to the growing number of families who want to keep their baby close to them at night. These devices look like playpens (and, indeed, many of them convert to playpens), but with only three walls and a mattress elevated to the same height as the parents' bed. The unit attaches to the bed securely so the baby won't fall through the cracks (literally) but can rest within handy distance to the nursing mom. Models range in price from $150 to $300. Some parents achieve the sidecar effect by removing the drop side of a crib and wedging the crib between their bed and a wall.

Cribs

Once the baby has outgrown his cradle, bassinet, or basket, it's time to move to a crib. Cribs have been under strict safety regulations since the 1980s, so you can rest assured that any new crib you buy in the United States will be safe. Here are the basic safety requirements, as stated by the U.S. Consumer Product Safety Commission.

- Crib slats should be no more than 2 ⅜" apart; make sure none is missing, loose, or cracked.
- The mattress should fit snugly (no more than two adult finger-widths

The bassinet usually ends up in the parents' room for convenience sake; consider choosing a fabric to match your room rather than the baby's.

should fit between the mattress and the crib's side).

- The mattress support should be firmly attached to both head and foot boards.
- Corner posts should be no more than ¹⁄₁₆" high.
- The head and foot boards should not have cutouts, which allow entrapment.
- The side-release latches should not be operable by the baby, and should securely hold the sides in the raised position.
- All hardware should be present and tight.
- No soft bedding—comforters, pillows, sheepskins—should be placed in the crib.
- The baby should be put to sleep on his back.

A Moses basket's manageable handles and light weight make it easy to move from room to room.

A few other things to look for: Is the crib sturdy or wobbly? Give it a few good pushes. If you are buying a metal bed, examine the welding closely, and run your hand over it—any sharp edges? Are the casters sturdy, and do they lock in place—or are they removable? (Active toddlers sometimes like to make their cribs "walk" across the room.)

Is the mattress support sturdy, and does it allow for air circulation? Some cribs have only vinyl straps or even cardboard supports; wood slats are sturdy, but offer little give; spring coils are a nice choice, and will be appreciated during the years of jumping on the bed.

Look at and ask about the finish. Luckily, lead paint was phased out in the late '70s (you shouldn't even consider using a crib of that vintage or earlier, even if it is a family heirloom). Still, the finish should be nontoxic and not prone to chipping. The more coats of nontoxic lacquer a crib has, the more gracefully it will take its inevitable beating.

Next, how does the side-release mechanism work? Some require the use of two hands spread an adult's arm-span apart, making it impossible for a baby or child to release. The downside to this type is that you can't operate it with a baby in your arms. Many cribs are moving to the lift-with-one-hand, push-with-knee action. This keeps one arm free for holding the baby, and the hardware is either invisible or minimally visible. The potential downside: a good-size sibling could open this without too much trouble.

Popular for years, and still found on some models, is the foot-release bar, which you press down with one foot while lowering the crib rail with one arm. This mechanism is falling out of favor, as the spring-loaded hardware is both visible and sometimes noisy, and too easy for even small kids to trigger. Less safe is the fold-down crib railing, which can pinch fingers (even limbs),

A sidecar sleeper keeps the newborn within arm's reach, making nighttime feedings less disruptive for everyone. Later, it converts to a playpen or travel bed.

and provide a foothold for babies to launch themselves out of the crib.

What about crib-mattress levels? While different models have as many as four levels, a practical, safety-minded parent would say only two are needed: a high position for before the baby is sitting or pulling up, and a very low position to last until the toddler reaches 35 inches in height or can climb or fall over the sides (signs that it's time to move to a regular bed). Also assess the frustration factor for the height-adjustment mechanism; lowering the mattress is one chore you won't want to procrastinate about.

Some cribs boast "convertibility." Remove one side and lower the mattress one last notch, and you have a so-called "junior" bed that uses the same crib bedding and looks like a little daybed. On others you unstack a dresser off the end, put on a longer mattress or mattress extension and have a "youth" bed, which requires sheets in a size that can be hard to find. In the end, most toddlers are quite ready to move directly from a crib to a new and exciting twin-size bed, and anything between is little more than a marketing gimmick.

The only other factors that separate the hundreds of cribs on the market are style, price, and quality. You can buy a crib for as little as $100 at a baby superstore, or pay up to $700 at a high-end shop. Styles range as much as in adult furniture. As this piece will probably be used the shortest length of time of any furniture in the nursery (except the cradle or bassinet), you may want to choose the style of dresser or armoire you like first, and pick the crib to coordinate with it (rather than the other way around). If you

This crib's distressed finish will make it look less violated by the bangs and bumps baby furniture must endure.

plan on using the crib for more than one child, it is probably worth spending a little more for extra sturdiness and a stronger finish. A word to the wise: Buy plastic teething covers for both side rails when you purchase the crib—babies start gnawing sooner than you think.

Crib mattresses

There are generally two types of crib mattresses to choose from: innerspring and foam, with a wide range of quality and firmness in both types. Prices run from $40 to $150, and you can pay upwards of $600 for an organic-cotton crib mattress. Some higher-end furniture stores sell only innersprings, claiming foam mattresses break down too quickly. But a quality foam mat-

tress will last a long time and can give better value than a cheap innerspring.

Whichever you choose, be certain it fits snugly in the crib you've chosen. Also, babies need good, firm support to prevent suffocation. If the mattress is foam, press your hand on it, and then see how quickly it regains its original shape. The heavier (denser) the foam, the longer the mattress should last. On an innerspring, check not only the number of steel coils but the thickness of the coils, and look for a border rod to give the edges support.

If you want the advantages of both foam and innerspring, seek out one of the new combination mattresses with dense foam on one side, for the baby months, and springs on the other side, for the toddler period.

Dressers and Changing Tables

WHEN IT'S TIME FOR A CHANGE, YOU'LL BE READY

While a tiny baby doesn't need a lot of furniture in those first months, you will definitely want a convenient, comfortable place to change diapers up to a dozen times a day. And even the tiniest clothes need to be stashed somewhere. Blankets, sheets, waterproof pads, and diapers need a home, too. Unless your nursery closet is spacious and outfitted with drawers or shelves, you'll probably need some sort of a dresser or armoire.

Diaper-changing surfaces

A changing table can lead a very short life. Even though some children wear diapers well into their fourth year, few parents bother hoisting them up onto a changing table beyond age two.

Luckily, the trend on the furniture side is away from short-use, stand-alone changing tables toward dual-purpose items—dressers whose tops start as changing tables and convert to hutches (or just plain dresser tops). You can pay as little as $100 for an assemble-it-yourself unit at a baby superstore, or as much as $700 for a high-end European model. Or you can create this effect yourself by simply using any hip-height dresser and fastening a contoured changing pad on top (they snap onto the back of the dresser with included hardware). Be sure that the dresser/pad combination is at a comfortable height for the person who will be changing the most diapers; bending over can be especially painful for new mothers who have had a cesarean-section delivery or epidural anesthetic.

The most important safety feature of a changing table is not straps or a raised side, as you might think; these features may lull you into a false sense of security when, in fact, you should never leave the changing table's side while your baby is on it. No, the most important precaution you can take is to have everything you need for the change within arm's reach—waterproof pads, clean diapers, a dirty-diaper bin, wipes or water, diaper creams, clean clothes. Be sure you arrange the space in and around the changing area to accommodate these supplies.

An option for families with a large bathroom counter is simply to make part of that room "diaper central." The surfaces are probably easier to clean, disposing of the diaper contents could not be handier, and warm water (a cheap, healthy cleanser for the baby's bottom) is in plentiful supply.

Finally, when you choose your changing pad, look for raised sides to keep your baby from rolling over in mid-change. Also, check on the availability of cloth covers. Do they come in colors that work for your nursery? Are they a standard size or by special order only? You'll want to have two or three covers, as well as a dozen or so small waterproof pads so you can place a fresh one on top for each change.

If the dresser you've chosen isn't at a comfortable changing height, you can buy a "deck" that will raise the pad and provide space for diapers and other change essentials underneath.

Dressers and armoires

When deciding on a dresser style, think not only about how much space you have but also about what you will put in it and how a child will use it. It will be used much longer than the crib, so choose with an eye to the future. You may even want to buy this piece at an "adult" furniture store. You can also get an inexpensive dresser at an unfinished furniture store, then paint or stain it to match your crib or other furniture you may already have

chosen. Spend a little extra on unique knobs, and you'll have a custom piece for a fraction of the price.

A low, double-wide bureau is a wise choice, as all the drawers are easy-access by age three (with the aid of a small step stool), when most kids start wanting to dress themselves. A highboy makes sense only if you are short on floor space and want to store things out of your child's reach; make sure any tall dresser is securely anchored to the wall.

Once the changing-table surface on this wall unit is no longer necessary, a second hutch can be added to the dresser. Here, corner shelves hold baby-soft gear. They can be added at any time.

An armoire can function as a closet while the baby's hanging clothes are few and small. In later years, it can be used as a media cabinet or for collection display and storage.

Think about how the dresser will function in the future. Some models are part of a set that allows you to add a hutch on top or a corner shelf unit (also called a "radius shelf") on either side. Your child's storage needs will only grow, so plan accordingly.

Armoires are an increasingly popular choice; in the baby years, the top cupboard is outfitted with a pole to hang small dresses or jackets, while the lower drawers store the rest of the clothes and blankets. Some parents start out with shelves in the top portion, leave the doors open, and use it as a display area for the baby's treasures. Later, the cupboard can store collections, books, or even a television.

Safety considerations include the obvious—is it sturdy and free of sharp edges?—and the not so obvious—are the drawer knobs or handles easy for small hands to get a grip on? Gliders or center guides will make drawers slide in and out more smoothly, making it easier for preschoolers to dress themselves and put away their clothes. Drawers that are heavy and quick to shut, however, are a recipe for pinched fingers. If your toddler is a climber, put safety locks on the drawers, or they may be used as steps (another reason to anchor the dresser to the wall). Finally, ensure that the drawers can't be removed altogether, or a toddler may end up pulling one out on top of himself.

Other items you may want to save space for in your child's room: a small table and chair set (it will be appreciated by 18 months of age), a miniature armchair for "reading" (even one-year-olds love to imitate Mom and Dad), and a nightstand for next to the rocking chair (until the "big bed" comes along).

Toddlers enjoy having a small table and chair. Be sure to buy the smallest-scale version available so a little guy can get on and off the chair himself with ease. Some sets come with interchangeable legs that allow the table to "grow" as the child does.

DIAPER DUTY

If you are using a cloth-diaper service, it will provide you with a diaper bin; for safety's sake, use only nontoxic deodorizer cakes to keep it smelling fresh. For those who use disposable diapers, one kind of bin actually seals each used diaper into a plastic sheath to cut down on odor. The device's downsides: Some parents find it complicated to use, the sheath refills are an ongoing expense (on top of the cost of diapers and the bin itself, about $30), and the sheaths add even more plastic to landfills. A lined deodorized pail with a childproof lid, emptied daily, is kind enough on most parents' noses.

Rocking Chairs

Rocker-gliders are available in hundreds of styles and upholstery choices. A nearby table keeps a reading light and telephone handy.

The baby's comfort quotient isn't the only one that matters—moms and dads will spend many hours throughout the day and night feeding and soothing their newborn, and a supportive, cozy chair makes everyone happier. Traditionally, rockers were the answer. But while their spindle back and wooden seat and arms look great, they're hardly what you want to sink into when you crawl out of bed for a middle-of-the-night feeding. Rocking chairs also have a tendency to travel across the floor as you rock them.

Step into any nursery furniture store and you'll see that some clever (or bone-weary) soul has come to the rescue with rocker-gliders. These heavily cushioned alternatives have a ball-bearing mechanism that lets you glide back and forth for hours with hardly any strain on the lower back.

All likely caregivers should try out the chair in the store. Be sure to choose a model with cushioned armrests, or you'll soon regret it. And an inclined footrest will angle the legs in a way that will help support the baby. Few of the gliding ottomans sold to match the chairs are comfortable if you're holding a baby, but they are a luxurious addition for future use.

Rocker-gliders are available in hundreds of styles, finishes, and upholstery choices to match any decor, from Shaker to contemporary. Rather than coordinating it with the nursery, many parents select a model that fits in with the master bedroom or whatever room the chair might be moved to later.

Not only is the chair likely to be the most comfortable seat in the house, it can also represent a significant investment: prices range from $100 for discount-store models to $1,000 for high-end, leather versions with swivel options, recline positions, even heated massage. Matching gliding ottomans can cost up to $430. As with cribs and other nursery furnishings, high-end gliders offer the best selection of styles and upholstery, but cost the most and require special ordering.

Some people prefer a simpler rocker. Luckily, more easy chairs are being "rocker-ized," like the two shown here. Again, look for good back support, a comfortable size, and an easy rocking motion.

Don't forget the most comfortable option of all (provided you have the space)—a daybed set up in the nursery to accommodate middle-of-the-night feedings.

Newer rocking chairs are both stylish and comfortable.

Shopping for Furniture:
Where to Go, What to Ask, How to Save

The baby boom has created an enormous market for all things baby. But the level of service, quality of merchandise, and prices will vary depending on where you shop.

Baby specialty retailers, for instance, range in size from independent mom-and-pop stores to small chains to high-end, national franchises. These stores usually carry mid- to high-quality brands—and relatively high prices. On the plus side, they are also more likely to offer a higher level of customer service.

You'll find more competitive prices, but less in the way of helpful advice, at baby superstores; these tend to carry not only furniture and bedding but also baby clothes, diapers, and accessories.

Many department stores—discount and traditional—are quite likely to have baby departments these days. The furniture selection is often more limited and the staff less knowledgeable than in specialty stores; price ranges vary, depending on the store. And don't forget regular furniture stores—the crib is the only item you'll really need that you won't find there.

Web sites and catalogs are popping up all over. Prices can be very reasonable, though bedding and accessories may be better buys than furniture, for which shipping costs can be prohibitive. You can't see and touch the merchandise before you buy, so find out as much as possible about the brand and quality by asking detailed questions of the customer-service representative before you place your order. Some companies will even send out fabric or finish samples for a refundable fee.

Another popular option for bargain hunters is secondhand furniture. While you can find good dressers, rockers, and smaller items this way, buying a used crib is risky business as it's very difficult to know if it meets current safety standards (see page 85). To find out if there have been any safety complaints about secondhand items you've been given or have found at garage sales or consignment stores, contact the U.S. Consumer Product Safety Commission at (800) 638-2772.

Wherever you shop, evaluate baby furniture as you would any other major purchase. First, find out what it is made of. Solid wood is most durable, but also most expensive; a good veneer can often match it in appearance and beat it in price. Composition board is less expensive, but more prone to chipping. Finally, laminates are very sturdy, colorful, easy to care for, and reasonably priced.

Ask yourself these questions: Is the piece solid and sturdy? Is it free of sharp edges and splinters? Is the hardware secure, and are the corners rounded? Do all the moving parts work well? Always inquire about the item's warranty and the store's return procedure. For expensive items, you may want to think twice about a store-credit-only policy.

Storage

WHERE TO STASH, STACK, AND STORE ALL THAT STUFF

A baby's belongings grow exponentially, so storage space is always at a premium. Closets, floor space, and wall space can all be used very efficiently, thanks to the boom in storage devices and planning services. Most of the items mentioned here can be found at specialty storage shops, home centers, and large discount outlets.

Closets

Chances are, your nursery closet was designed for an adult's clothes and has one long pole hanging about five feet above the floor, with perhaps one shelf above that. Whether you do it yourself or hire a closet-organizing service (look under Closet Accessories in the yellow pages), you can make the space work more efficiently for your baby.

Early on you will need only one small pole for hanging clothes, and then only if you have a little girl with dresses. The pole's height should be adjustable, so that once your child is old enough to put clothes on a hanger (two to three years) she can reach to put them away herself.

Install shelves or sliding wire drawers on glider tracks below or next to the pole. Hang a clear shoe-storage bag over the back of the closet door for shoes, socks, hats, and other small items that are easily lost.

Save some space in the closet to store clothes, equipment, or toys that the child has outgrown (if you are sav-

One side of a double-wide closet has been fitted with an efficient combination of pull-out wire bins (for toys), drawers (for clothes), and shelves. A hanging mesh bag catches the baby's laundry items. The other side of the closet has more shelves, as well as two levels of hanging space.

ing them for another baby) as well as the clothes he has yet to grow into. Also, keep a large, clear plastic bin in the closet for toys that you "rotate" off the shelves in your baby's room every month or so; when you bring them back out, they'll shine like new again.

Shelves and bookcases

Bookcases, though one of the most practical furniture items a parent can invest in, are seldom sold as part of nursery furniture sets—yet another reason to shop at adult or unfinished furniture stores. The longer you intend to keep the shelves, the more durable you'll want them, and the more you may have to pay. Solid hardwood will hold up better in the long run than less expensive laminates or veneers.

As with dressers, if floor space is at a minimum, go for height (and be sure to anchor the bookcase to the wall). You'll want easily adjustable shelves, as toys and books range and change in size over the years. A 12- to 14-inch depth will accommodate most toys and books, yet is not so deep that things get lost.

Built-in shelving allows you to maximize space from floor to ceiling, and from wall to wall. Modular units—combinations of shelves, cupboards, and drawers—are often available in a wide enough range of sizes to offer the look and function of built-ins at a fraction of the cost and with much more flexibility. They are sold at many value-oriented furniture stores.

While closed cupboards may keep clutter out of sight, they make it harder for a toddler to see, get out, and put away his toys easily. Open baskets, bins, or clear shoe- or sweater-storage

Lightweight plastic bins of varying sizes can slide out and be set on the floor; small, wall-mounted drawers are painted in colors to coordinate. The strip of wall-mounted peg rack acts as a dado molding, separating zones of contrasting wall color.

Peg racks can be simple or decorative; use them to hang clothes, hats, or toys. Mount them at least 36 inches off the ground to be above eye-injury height.

CD shelves are the perfect size for a baby's board books and small toys.

boxes on low shelves are easy to find and actually make maintaining order easier. Label containers with a picture of their contents to make them even more child-legible.

On the walls

Wall space can provide another dimension to your storage solutions. In addition to being practical, a variety of wall shelves, peg racks, and display cupboards add a decorative element.

Small, high shelves are ideal for displaying framed photos, and glass-fronted display cupboards are a dust-free way to show off precious collectibles and mementos. Peg racks can be purchased everywhere from hardware outlet stores to baby-furniture boutiques, depending on whether you want plain and practical or cute and decorative. Use them to hang sweaters, bonnets, and christening gowns, or to hang drawstring bags full of toys.

Toy chests

While many parents-to-be think a toy chest is a nursery essential, this notion is mostly nostalgia. In fact, toy chests are more like toy "black holes": They are deep and big, and encourage disorder. They are great, however, for storing baby blankets or linens.

An important safety note: Heirloom toy chests and chests not designed for children's use can actually be haz-

ardous, as the lids can slam down on fingers (and heads) and can entrap children. As you evaluate toy chests, look for ventilation holes, lids that are free of latches, and hinges that are spring-loaded to support the lid open in any position. Corner risers that create a finger space between the lid and the box are also recommended.

Lidless, lightweight plastic wastebaskets can be carried from room to room, and make cleanup a snap.

A handpainted toy chest is a beautiful addition to the nursery, and brings visual storytelling to a crawler's eye level.

Crib Bedding

PRACTICAL CONSIDERATIONS FOR THIS FABRIC FOCAL POINT

The linens available for cribs today are so lively and appealing that they can easily serve as the foundation for a nursery's decor. In fact, many companies offer everything from lamp shades to height-measuring sticks to stencil patterns that coordinate with their bedding lines. The trick is to rein yourself in and be sure your choices are safe and sensible.

The basics

What exactly do you need, and what should you look for? On the minimalist end, you will need three or four crib sheets and a few light crib blankets. A bumper isn't really necessary, and should be taken out of the crib as soon as the baby is sitting or pulling up, usually by around five or six months. Sheets should be generously cut to allow for shrinkage, as too-small sheets can slip off the mattress and entangle the baby. For the same reason, they should have good-quality elastic all around, not just on the corners. Make sure the sheet fits snugly and remains tucked under at all times. Cotton, knit, or flannel—it's up to you, but put baby's safety and comfort first.

The best crib blankets aren't the fluffy comforters sold in many bedding sets. In fact, because of the more than 1,000 crib deaths per year associated with suffocation, the U.S. Consumer Product Safety Commission recommends keeping fluffy bedding,

Translucent plastic in this space-theme crib mobile plays with light, casting rainbows around the room.

There's no rule saying infant bedding must be in pastels; babies also appreciate bold, high-contrast colors and patterns.

Soft, friendly creatures gaze downward at the baby from a wind-up musical mobile.

pillows, and stuffed animals, out of the crib altogether for the first year. (Comforters often end up being used on the floor or hung on the wall as decoration.) Temperature-appropriate pajamas or sleepers are the best covering, but if you must use a blanket, choose one that is lightweight and loosely woven, and tuck it under the mattress so that it covers only up to the infant's chest. Make sure your baby's head remains uncovered while sleeping.

Bedding sets

Most coordinated bedding sets come with a fitted sheet, a bumper, a bed skirt, and a blanket, coverlet, comforter, or duvet cover. (Remember, soft bedding is not to be used in the crib during the first year.) Most juvenile-furnishings stores charge from $150 to $250 for these sets, though they can be found for less at cut-rate department stores and baby superstores. Inspect each of the items individually, and be sure you can buy extra fitted sheets that will look attractive with the set. Also, keep an eye out for bedding sets

with so-called "summer blankets"—these match the set but have no filling, so they pose less risk of suffocation.

You can also buy sets by the piece from linen catalogs, children's furnishings catalogs, and the increasing number of home stores offering baby lines. There is also the special-order option, available at most juvenile furniture stores, which will net you the greatest range of styles and, in many cases, better quality than off-the-shelf sets. Expect to pay between $300 and $700 for special-order or custom bedding.

Some quality checkpoints: Is the fabric prewashed for shrinkage and softness? Is the pattern printed on or stamped on? (If the latter, it will fade more quickly.) How tight is the stitching? If there are appliqués, are they secure? Are the bumper ties sewn on tightly, and on both the top and bottom of the bumper (and are there at least 12 bumper ties)? Is the bumper washable, or does it have to be dry-cleaned? Some high-end

bumpers and comforters come with removable covers for easy washing.

Chances are, if you pay a little more for a higher-quality product, it will look better and last longer. Remember, you will launder this bedding more than most, and may use it for more than one baby (one reason to choose a gender-neutral set you really love).

Mobiles

Hung above nearly every crib (and most changing tables) is a twirling, cheerful, and sometimes musical mobile to entertain the baby. While these are often sold to match bedding sets, a mobile is more than just a nursery accessory. It's the baby's first toy and should be at least as functional as it is attractive.

The primary consideration should be: How will this look to the occupant of the crib? View it from underneath. The best mobile designs have the decorations angled downward so the baby gets the full visual impact. A musical option is nice too.

A versatile, C-shaped cushion is an ideal nursing pillow, as well as a supportive first chair and prop for the baby.

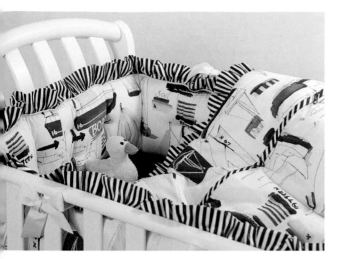

Crib sets come in every pattern and palette

imaginable. And if you can't find what you

want in a store or catalog, it can always be

custom-made in the fabric of your choice.

Wall Treatments

TURN A BLANK CANVAS INTO A COLORFUL BACKDROP

Yellow and white stripes below are separated from the stars and swirls above by a glued-on strip of ball fringe.

Walls can be a simple background for the nursery's other highlights. Or they can be the room's focal point, setting the theme with an elaborate mural or whimsical wallpaper. Whichever you choose, the finish should be nontoxic and easy to clean.

Paint

A fresh coat of paint in just the right shade can change a room's look overnight. While color is the main paint question parents ponder, there are important safety issues to consider, too. First, if your house was built before 1978, when lead-base paint was banned in this country, have the walls and trim checked for lead by a professional or by using a home test kit. Lead poisoning is a serious danger for adults, children, and even a fetus. If lead is detected, call the Lead Information Center and Clearinghouse at (800) 532-3394 for information on how to proceed.

Next, which finish and type of paint should you choose? Most parents select a water-base latex in a wipeable eggshell finish for the walls, and a durable, easy-to-wash semigloss finish for the trim. Water-base paints are not only less smelly than their oil-base counterparts, they are also quick and easy to apply, and they dry faster.

Because of increased awareness about the harmful effects of solvents, more and more parents are choosing not only paints that are water-base latex (which have less solvent in them than oil-base formulations) but also those labeled "Low VOC" or "No VOC" (for

Rubber stamps dipped in colorful acrylic paints are easy enough for the most amateur decorator to create effective designs.

volatile organic compounds). Most paint stores carry these health- and environment-friendly products in the same range of colors as regular paints. Whatever product you choose, paint the nursery at least a month before the baby is due, and allow plenty of ventilation during and after painting.

Decorative painting

A baby's room seems the perfect place for a mural or stencil treatment. An increasing number of professional muralists are offering their services; word of mouth is the best source, followed by references from baby-furnishings stores. College art students are a less expensive alternative. There are also paint-by-number mural transfer kits that give professional-looking results to the most amateur painter. Rubber stamps dipped in acrylic craft paints are perhaps the simplest and quickest way to give walls an individualized treatment.

One money-saving approach that will make changes easier down the road: Limit the mural to one wall, and paint the other walls in the background color or a complementary shade.

Wallpaper

Another way to jazz up nursery walls is with colorful wallpapers or borders. If you've already selected the bedding, window coverings, or trim paint, be

Crawlers appreciate it when an engaging mural comes down to their level.

sure to bring samples or swatches with you when you go to the wallpaper store. Bring along room measurements, too, so you can get an accurate estimate of how much paper you'll need.

Vinyl wallpaper is most durable and the easiest to clean, but it can harbor mildew in hot, humid climates with air conditioning. Coated paper is also wipeable, but be sure to ask about recommended cleaning procedures. Uncoated paper wallpaper isn't practical for a nursery or child's room. If you haven't wallpapered before and/or

your walls are uneven (as they are in many older houses), you may want professional installation.

Wallpaper borders are an even simpler way to bring pattern to nursery walls. Though often applied where the walls meet the ceiling, mounting them lower on the wall provides more fun for the baby. Some parents apply the border about 30 inches from the floor, or about where a chair rail would be, and either use different colors above and below it or apply an easy-to-clean paint below and wallpaper above.

As with paints, ask store salespeople or your installation expert about using low-VOC adhesives, and allow at least a few days for the room to air out after application.

Wall accessories

Plain walls can be dressed up easily with all manner of pictures, framed photos, and cloth wall hangings (here's your chance to display the quilt or comforter that can't be used in the baby's crib). Make sure whatever you hang is secured to the wall firmly; anything hung above the crib should be extremely lightweight (consider decorative paper plates or printed fabric).

Posters or fancy sheets of gift wrap laminated on pressboard give a finished, easy-to-wipe look without glass; most frame shops offer this service—and charge less for it than for regular framing.

Nursery no-nos

While chalkboard paint and corkboard walls are great choices for older children, they're unsafe for babies. Chalk and chalk dust are too likely to be ingested, and the tacks used to attach things to cork walls are a hazard.

Borders and wallpaper can be mixed and matched or used on their own to bring life to dull walls.

A WORD ON CHILDREN AND ENVIRONMENTAL TOXINS

More and more research is being done on the potential effects of toxins in everything from paint to wallpaper adhesives to carpet backing to new furniture. While the verdict is still out on many issues, it is clear that babies are the most vulnerable population for adverse reactions, for a number of reasons. Their

organs and systems are not yet fully developed; they take in more air in proportion to their body weight than do adults; they spend more time close to the ground where toxicants in dust and carpets settle; and their hand-to-mouth behavior creates pathways for exposure to toxicants, especially lead in paint chips or pesticide residues.

If you are interested in learning more about making healthy choices consult the resources on Children's Environmental Health Network's Web site, www.cehn.org, contact Mothers and Others for a Livable Planet at www.mothers.org, or check the Washington Toxics Coalition at www.accessone.com/~watoxics.

Flooring

Babies spend a lot of their first two years on the floor—crawling, playing, and yes, falling. You'll want a surface that's hospitable to the little one's various activities but also easy to keep clean. While carpeting is soft for crawlers, most types are not suitable for, say, building block towers. It also stains easily and traps dust mites and residues tracked in on shoes. Wood floors and resilient surfaces, such as vinyl and cork, are better for play and far easier to keep clean, but offer little cushion for a fall. That's why most experts recommend a combination of hard or resilient surfacing with one or two small rugs or a carpeted area.

Resilient surfaces

Though often associated with kitchens and bathrooms, vinyl, linoleum, cork, and rubber are also good choices for the nursery, as they are hard-wearing, easy to clean, and softer than wood. Sealed cork is especially practical, as it is sound-absorbing as well as soft

Stenciled numbers and letters add a playful element to Douglas fir flooring, above. The primary colors blend well with children's toys and bedding, and the random pattern provides flexibility in arranging the furniture. Resilient flooring (below, left) can be cut and fit together seamlessly into playful patterns and color combinations, either wall to wall or as an area "rug." Playful interlocking rubber "puzzle" tiles cushion falls (below, right). The tiles come up easily and can be configured to fit any room shape. Edging pieces are available.

underfoot. Available in tiles or sheets, it is relatively easy to install.

Vinyl is another resilient flooring, especially appealing for the array of colors and patterns available. Cushion-backed vinyl is softer underfoot but may dent under heavy furniture or with a child's playful abuse. Inlaid patterns wear longer than photographically printed patterns. Be sure to ask about the protective finish on any vinyl you consider, as well as cleaning requirements (some have to be waxed, while others have an easy-care finish). Some vinyls must be professionally installed; others you can install yourself. Costs vary from about $4 to $40 per yard, not including installation.

Wood floors

Warm and appealing in its look, wood is a natural choice. Though a bare wood floor can be noisy, an area rug here and there will quiet things down, as well as add color and softness. If the nursery already has wood floors, make

sure they are splinter-free. Fill any cracks or spaces between boards, or they will attract crumbs, dirt, beads, and siblings' other very small toys.

If the floors are in rough shape and you'd like to refinish them, again look for low VOC-content products. Alternatively, you could sand the rough spots and paint the floor in a geometric pattern, or add a stenciled border. Be sure to apply a top coat of sealer for easier cleaning.

Carpet

While wall-to-wall carpet seems like a soft, quiet solution for the nursery, spills and spit-ups create hard-to-remove stains, and dust settles in too deeply for most vacuums to extract. The latter is especially problematic for babies with allergies or asthma. If you are nevertheless set on wall-to-wall carpeting, choose a very low pile, a loop carpet, or commercial-grade carpet. Consider a border of a different color and texture to appeal to a baby's developing tactile and visual senses; composing a pattern from an array of carpet squares can also add interest.

Sculpted carpet can be made into area rugs, as shown here, or be designed for wall-to-wall installation.

When choosing carpets, inquire about which is most stain resistant and easiest to clean, and least allergenic. Nylon often fits that bill, in addition to being less prone to pilling and static electricity. Be sure to use padding under it, not only to cushion falls but also to protect the carpet itself and the flooring.

As with paint and wallpaper, the backing, foam, dyes, insecticides, and adhesives used in carpet and installation often off-gas VOCs (volatile organic compounds). If this is a concern for you, shop for environmental and health-friendly natural floor coverings and

pads. Install carpet with tacks rather than glue, do the job as far in advance of the baby's arrival as possible, and let the nursery air out with open windows for at least 72 hours.

Area rugs

Throw rugs and larger area rugs are available in many nursery-appropriate colors and designs. Look not only in baby furnishings stores but also in home-furnishing and bed-linen catalogs and stores.

Hooked rugs offer the most detail and wonderful colors, and even come in whimsical shapes; most of them are made of cotton or nylon. Check with the manufacturer about cleaning procedures. The old braided rugs are back, in brighter colors, in wonderfully soft chenille; they come in a wide range of sizes, in both oval and round shapes. And don't forget thick bathroom throw mats that come in every color towels do and couldn't be easier to clean.

Whichever rug you choose to soften up an area of the floor, be sure to leave some hard surfacing for racing cars, floor puzzles, and the like. Also, use a nonslip pad to keep the rug in place.

Low-pile or looped carpet in patterns (left) adds visual interest underfoot and helps mask stains. Hooked rugs (right) come in a fanciful array of motifs and colors. Be sure to use nonslip pads underneath them.

Window Treatments

FANCIFUL WAYS TO DARKEN A ROOM DURING THE DAY

Window coverings in the nursery not only help modulate the light (important for those early afternoon naps) but add a decorative element, too. Balancing the two jobs is easy, given the abundance of choices and their mix- and match-ability. As always, safety is a top concern, especially when it comes to the cords and pulls associated with many window coverings. Also think about ease of cleaning, as you will have less time but more messes on your hands once you become a parent.

When you head to the store, be sure to bring detailed measurements of your nursery windows; photos will help when it comes to describing exactly where the coverings will be installed, and which measurements apply to what areas. If climate control is an issue where you live, ask about the window covering's R-value, which indicates a product's resistance to heat loss (the higher the R-value, the more complete the insulation).

Blinds

Wooden-slat blinds are more traditional and and give better insulation, while metal and plastic look crisp and contemporary and are less expensive. All types are relatively easy to keep clean. One caution: Replace any imported vinyl miniblinds made before the summer of 1996, as these have been found to contain lead.

An odd-shaped window gets special treatment with a custom wrought-iron curtain rod and custom painted-linen curtains that follow the window's curve. A button-out blackout lining blocks strong eastern light and is removed easily when it's time to launder the curtains.

A valance is accented with painted letters spelling out the child's name (top). Traditional wood-slat blinds (above) make it easy to modulate light; their clean lines are softened with a button-trimmed valance.

Blackout blinds hang behind the Roman shade-like valance on the terrace door and also behind the cornice on the arched window above the terrace door.

If you have standard-size windows, you may find off-the-shelf blinds to fit; otherwise, you'll have to special-order them (delivery rarely takes more than a week or two). While blinds come in a wide range of colors, the most sensible choice is to match the window trim. You can hide the hardware for the blinds and add color and pattern with a cloth valance or boxlike, fabric-covered cornice.

Remember, blinds' cords present a choking hazard: wrap excess cord tightly around a cord cleat fixed as high on the window frame as the shortest adult can reach.

Shades

Choices here range from a simple roller shade to custom-made Roman or balloon shades to the newer cellular shades. Roller shades are the least expensive, and can be dressed up with iron-on fabric, wallpaper, or even painted designs (use fabric paints). Kids may be tempted to toy with the auto-release mechanism on some shades; choosing a pulley system will make this less attractive. On a pulley system, though, be sure to have the continuous-loop chain cut short enough so it can't be reached by children.

Blackout shades have an inner layer that keeps light from penetrating, giving a nightlike feel to a room for daytime sleeping. Be sure these shades are cut generously enough so rays don't sneak in from the sides or bottom of the shade.

Curtains

While curtains and draperies can really dress up a window, they are the least practical option in a nursery. They tend to be harder to clean than blinds or shades; and because they gather more dust, they can be especially aggravating for allergy- or asthma-prone children. They are also tempting for little ones to play with and hang on.

Lighting

BRIGHT IDEAS FOR ILLUMINATING THE ROOM

For your sake as well as your baby's, think carefully about the nursery's lighting. You will want to be able to check on your sleepyhead without waking him, as well as have adequate light for story reading and playtime. Because lights involve both hot bulbs and electricity, safety is, again, a primary concern.

You'll find suitable light fixtures at a range of suppliers. Juvenile-furnishings boutiques will have the widest array of child-oriented lamps, while general lighting stores will offer a wider range of ceiling fixtures in simple styles that would be fine for a nursery and would adapt well to a child's room. Specialty lighting and juvenile-furnishings catalogs are another source of lamps and light fixtures.

When choosing lights for the nursery, stick with those that accept regular incandescent bulbs. Halogen bulbs, while long-lasting, burn dangerously hot and produce too bright a light for babies. Also consider the light switch: Will it be easy for a small hand to operate? While initially you may not appreciate a toddler's frequent on-and-off-with-the-lights games (a product of their fascination with cause and effect), there will soon come a day when you appreciate their independence in such small tasks.

Ceiling fixtures

Overhead fixtures are the safest light source in a nursery since the wiring is behind walls and the fixture itself is well out of the baby's reach. Choose a fixture style with a shade that covers the bulb and softens the light; babies spend a lot of time staring at the ceiling, and untamed bulbs can be harsh on young eyes. Some shades have glow-in-the-dark designs that linger long after lights-out, giving the baby something to gaze at.

If you are having several recessed lights installed, consider having several switches so that the lights can be operated independently. And whether you have one overhead light or several, be sure to install a dimmer switch to make it easy to check on the baby at night without rousing him.

Wall fixtures

Sconces and wall fixtures provide more localized lighting than an overhead fixture. They are safer than table lamps because they aren't easily knocked over, but chances are they are reachable by a determined toddler, so teach your child a healthy respect for hot bulbs early on.

Ideally, wall lights are hard-wired into the wall so there are no cords hanging loose. If that's not possible, hang the fixture as close to the outlet as possible and secure the cords in

Table lamps can be dressed up with shades hand-decorated to reflect the room's look.

This low-wattage lamp's colored insert rotates slowly, creating moving pictures on darkened walls.

Lamps like this one are often sold as part of a bedding collection.

This tea-party chandelier makes the room's primary light source a decorative focal point.

A ceramic ceiling fixture features star cutouts—a subtle, gender-neutral touch.

covers adhered to the wall (some people use duct tape or masking tape painted the color of the wall).

Freestanding lamps

Table lamps come in a wide range of nursery-appropriate styles; many are designed to match bedding sets or have juvenile themes. Some are made of ceramic, others of painted wood, and still others are crafted from antique toys. In some cases, the lamp base is the decorative centerpiece, while other lamps feature a clever shade.

While nursery table lamps are decorative, they can also be dangerous. Ideally, they sit out of reach on a table that blocks the outlet they are plugged into; excess cord should be gathered on a cord winder. For extra safety, consider screwing the lamp onto the table or dresser.

Floor lamps are an option only for older children.

Nightlights

Recent studies suggest that a nightlight (or any dim light) left on all night in a room occupied by a baby under two may be related to later myopia (nearsightedness). While the research still needs follow-up, the evidence is compelling enough to suggest that a nightlight is appropriate for the hallway, but not the nursery (unless it is turned off once the baby falls asleep). All the more reason to put the main light on a dimmer that you can regulate as you enter and leave the room. If you do use a nightlight, be sure to locate it well away from any flammable materials, and consider using nightlights that have cooler neon minibulbs, rather than 4- or 7-watt bulbs.

Wall-mounted lamps can provide soft indirect light (sailboat) or act as reading lights (gooseneck and beaded hat).

Safety

HOW TO KEEP THE NURSERY HAZARD-FREE

With a safety gate mounted on the outside, a terrace door can be opened for fresh air without any worry that the terrace's wrought-iron railing will be climbed. The knob cover provides an extra measure of security.

The good news about home safety is that most childhood injuries are actually preventable through a combination of good sense, safety devices, and supervision. While you can hire "baby proofers" to come into your home and secure it Fort Knox-style, you can probably accomplish the same thing yourself for a fraction of the cost and find most of the products at home centers, drugstores, mail-order catalogs, and baby-oriented Web sites.

When evaluating safety equipment, remember that in order to be effective it must be used. Is installation relatively simple? Will the device work on the intended door, cabinet, or drawer? Is it easy enough for older siblings to use and resecure? Assume your toddler will test the device: Will it withstand these assaults? If the answer to any of these questions is no, choose another model. And keep your receipts: Safety devices are notorious for working in a limited range of situations.

The gear recommended on these pages is limited in scope to nursery safety; consult baby-care books or the U.S. Consumer Product Safety Commission's Web site (www.cpsc.gov) for information on the rest of the house.

SAFETY LATCHES AND LOCKS are for cabinets, closets, and drawers, or anywhere you keep items that could be hazardous to babies, including medicines, scissors, fire ladders, and so on. Doorknob covers are another way to keep small children out of closets.

An adjustable bracket secures a bookshelf to the wall, but allows some movement in case of earthquake.

SAFETY GATES can be used to keep a baby from wandering during a play period or after a nap (if the crib no longer does the job). They can also be installed in window frames above the first floor to prevent dangerous falls (or look for special window guards). When evaluating a safety gate, be sure slats are vertical so they can't become toeholds. Those that are mounted onto the walls are safer than pressure gates, especially in windows and at the tops of stairs. The latch should be easy for an adult to operate. Look for a seal of approval from the Juvenile Products Manufacturers Association (JPMA).

A SMOKE DETECTOR should be installed just outside the nursery (in fact, outside every sleeping area in the home). Be sure to check the battery monthly and replace it annually, or use a 10-year battery.

A CARBON MONOXIDE ALARM should be placed outside the baby's room if you have gas or oil heat or an attached garage. Be sure the device meets requirements of the most recent UL standard 2034 or International Approval Services standard 696.

OUTLET COVERS are a must to prevent shock and electrocution. If you use outlet plugs, make sure they are UL-listed and cannot be easily removed or choked on. Because it is so

Smoke and fire detectors (far left) should be mounted either inside or just outside of the nursery. A sliding safety latch mounted on the bifold closet door (top left) keeps the doors closed and fingers from being pinched. Mounted sliding outlet covers (bottom left) are easy for parents to use, but keep paper clips and small fingertips out.

easy to misuse these plugs (take one out to plug something in, then never replace it), a better choice might be to install outlet plates that require a left-sliding motion to plug in a cord. If you won't need the outlet, replace the face with a blank plate. If you are concerned about your child pulling a cord out of the outlet, look for outlet and plug hoods that prevent this.

WINDOW-BLIND CORDS should be cut if they are looped, to prevent strangulation (remove the buckle as well); put safety tassels on the cut ends. Use cord cleats high on the window frame to take up excess cord. If you are buying new window coverings, inform the salesperson that you would like to have safety options on the cords.

L-BRACKETS, available at hardware stores, will secure tall or tip-prone dressers and bookcases to the wall—essential if you have a "climber." If you live in an area prone to earthquakes, look for a hinged model.

A BABY MONITOR will alert you when a sleeping baby awakens or otherwise needs you. Monitors in which both the base unit and the receiver can be powered by either household current or a battery give you the most flexibility.

A CORDLESS PHONE is an invaluable safety device, as it allows you to supervise your child even when callers beckon.

If you are concerned about a product's safety—especially if you are buying a used item—the U.S. Consumer Product Safety Commission lists all product recalls since 1994 on their Web site at www.cpsc.gov; or call (800) 638-2772 for recorded messages or a live operator.

design credits

FRONT MATTER

1.Muralist: Roxane Murphy Smith. 2. Design: Bellini. Decorative Artist: Lisa Besancon. 4 (bottom). Design: Bellini, Butera. Decorative Artist: Audrey Busby. 5. Interior Design: Elizabeth Benefield.

**CHAPTER ONE/
A PLANNING PRIMER**

6. Design: Bridget Baskett-Stone and Steve Stone. 7. Hearthsong

The Master Plan

8 (tape measure) Rockridge Kids. 8. Interior Design: Claire L. Sommers/McCabe & Sommers Interiors. 9. Interior Design: Lynz Designs & Associates/Lynda Pratt Notaro. 10-11. Design by Heija Tabb Nunn. 13. Go to Your Room.

14-15. Interior Design: Juvenile Lifestyles, Inc./Norm Claybaugh. Muralist: Rebecca. 17. Interior Design: David Weatherford Antiques and Interiors/Lori Broznowski. 18. Interior Design: Barbara McQueen Interior Design. 19. Muralist: Betts Art/ Todd Betts.

A Safe Haven

20 (monitor). Rockridge Kids. 20 (gate). Design and fabrication: Paul La Bruna. 21 (bottom right). Muralist: Sherrill Hull. 21 (top right). Window Treatment: Mara Rigel.

A Look That Will Last

22-23. Interior Design and Design Collage: David Weatherford Antiques and Interiors/ Lori Broznowski. 24. Muralist: Quinn

Art/Jeannie Lovell. 25. Interior Design: David Dalton Associates. 26. Interior Design: Juvenile Lifestyles, Inc/ Norm Claybaugh .

**CHAPTER TWO/
GREAT BABY ROOM IDEAS**

28. Interior Design: Little Folk Art/ Susan Salzman

Tying it all Together

30 (top). Bear: Goodnight Room. Blocks: Rockridge Kids. 30-31. Artisan: Heidi Favour. 32-33. Design: Cathleen Waronker and Melissa Dietz with Susan Salzman/Little Folk Art. Upholsterer: Lillian Leygerer. 34-35. Design: Little Folk Art/ Susan Salzman. 36-37. Interior Design: Mary Engelbreit's Studio. 38-39. Artist: Catherine Richards.

Murals and Color

40 (top). Rockridge Kids. 40-41. Interior Design: Juvenile Lifestyles, Inc./Norm Claybaugh. 42-43. Decorative Artist: Cheryl Mussman Smith. 44. Interior Design: City Studios. 45. Design: Sasha Emerson Levin. 46-47. Muralist: Betts Art/ Todd Betts. 48-49. Interior Design: Juvenile Lifestyles, Inc./Norm Claybaugh. Muralist: Debbra. 50-51. Muralist: Betts Art/ Todd Betts. 52-53. Muralist: Betts Art/ Todd Betts. 54. Muralist: Quinn Art/Jeannie Lovell. 55. Muralists: Art 4 Architecture/ Constance Scott and Sara Winchester. 56-57. Muralist: Janet White.

Small Wonders

58 (top). Dollhouse furniture: Sweet Dreams. Teapot: Rockridge Kids. 58. Interior Design: Erin Blake. 59. Design: Laurie McCartney for www.babystyle.com. 60. Design: Victoria Havlish. 61. Interior Design by Kathryn Hill Interiors. 62 (top). Goodnight Moon

Furniture and Accessories for A Child's Home. 62 (bottom). Design: Rosetree Cottage Interiors/Furnishings. Muralist: Roxane Murphy Smith. 63. Interior Designer: Jennifer Morgan Peterson.

Peas in a Pod

64 (top). Goodnight Room. 64-65. Design: Valerie Rostek. 66. Design and fabrication of changing units: Paul La Bruna. 67. Stenciling: Susan Griffin. 68. Muralist: Jennifer Carrasco. 69. Melissa Beyeler with design consultant Heather Stone for Imagine That.

Comfort Counts

70 (top) Bellini. 71. Goodnight Moon Furniture and Accessories for A Child's Home. 72. Muralist: Demar Feldman Studios/Miriam Feldman. Furniture from Imagine That. 73. Little Folk Art/ Susan Salzman. 74 (top). Design: Cindy Lorensen. 74 (bottom). Design: Rosetree Cottage Interiors/Furnishings. Muralist: Roxane Murphy Smith. 75. Design: Viola Lee Icken and Bill Icken/Icken Associates Inc.

Clutter Control

76 (top). Hearthsong, Rockridge Kids, Goodnight Room, Cotton and Co. 76. Melissa Beyeler with design consultant Heather Stone for Imagine That. 77. Goodnight Moon Furniture and Accessories for A Child's Home. 78-79. Design and fabrication: Holly Opfelt. Chenille stacking pillows: Baby Rose. 80. Design: Bridget Baskett-Stone and Steve Stone. 81 (top). Interior Design: McCabe & Sommers Interiors/ Claire L. Sommers. 81 (bottom). Melissa Beyeler with design consultant Heather Stone for Imagine That.

CHAPTER THREE/
A SHOPPER'S GUIDE

PHOTOGRAPHERS

Unless noted, all photographs are by E. Andrew McKinney.
Brad Bartholomew: 98 (bottom).
Larry Hawley: 86 (bottom).
Oleg March: 75.
Barbara Elliot Martin, courtesy of Mary Engelbreit's Children's Companion: 36-37.
Sibila Savage: 4 (top), 7, 8 (top), 20 (top), 27 (bottom), 30 (top), 40 (top), 58 (top), 64 (top), 76 (top), 83, 93.

index

Page numbers in **boldface** refer to photographs